D1598559

A.C.E.S. for Students: Strategies for Success in the First Year of College & Beyond

TRACY G. CRUMP, PHD, JD, LLM

Àṣẹ Publishing Group, LLC™

Published in the United States of America by Àṣẹ Publishing Group,
LLC™

First Edition

ISBN 979-8-218-12792-3 (Paperback)
ISBN 979-8-9876311-1-9 (E-Book)

Cover designed by Ida Fia Sveningsson
Author photo by Devon Kidd
Developmental Editor English Editorial
Line/Copy Editor & Proofreader Jodi Brandon Editorial

Printed in the United States of America.

www.tracycrumpenterprisesllc.com
www.tracygcrump.com
www.asepublishinggroup.com

Publisher's Cataloging-in-Publication
(Provided by Cassidy Cataloguing Services, Inc.).

Names: Crump, Tracy G., author.

Title: A.C.E.S. for students : strategies for success in the first year of college & beyond / Tracy G. Crump,
          PHD, JD, LLM.

Description: First edition. | [Chicago, Illinois] : Àṣẹ Publishing Group, LLC, [2023] | Includes
               bibliographical references and index.

Identifiers: ISBN: 979-8-218-12792-3 (Paperback) | 979-8-9876311-1-9 (E-Book) | LCCN:
               2023903061

Subjects: LCSH: College students--United States. | College student orientation--United States. |
             Academic achievement--United States. | Underprepared college students--United States. |
             Student adjustment--United States. | College environment--United States. | College students--
             United States--Conduct of life. | Motivation (Psychology) | Learning, Psychology of. | Self-
             realization. | Success. | Self-actualization (Psychology) | LCGFT: Instructional and
             educational works. | Study guides. | Self-help publications. | BISAC: EDUCATION / Student
             Life & Student Affairs. | EDUCATION / Professional Development. | EDUCATION / Learning
             Styles. | STUDY AIDS / College Entrance. | STUDY AIDS / College Guides. | STUDY AIDS /
             Study & Test-Taking Skills. | STUDY AIDS / Study Guides. | YOUNG ADULT NONFICTION /
             Study Aids / Test Preparation.

Classification: LCC: LC148.2 .C78 2023 | DDC: 378.1/619--dc23

Disclaimer

To all the barrier breakers and bridge builders whose
shoulders I stand on

and

Correy Sr., Bianca, and Correy II
who continue to be my north stars, muses, and the lights
guiding me home.

Contents

Preface
BUCKLE UP! Let's go

Preparing for college is a years-long process that will require you and your family to research potential colleges and universities to find the best fit; prepare for standardized examinations such as the SAT or ACT; develop sustainable, strong study habits; understand financial aid options, including scholarships, grants, and loans; and create a budget plan for managing expenses while attending college.

College readiness is an essential concept for any student looking to attend college. *A.C.E.S. for Students: Strategies for Success in the First Year of College & Beyond* aims to provide a comprehensive overview of the various steps and considerations necessary for successful college preparedness and college navigation during the first year of college and to provide you with a strong foundation of transferable skills that will assist you in the future.

When researching potential colleges and universities, you must clearly know what you need to succeed during your post-secondary education. It would help to consider the academic programs offered, the school's location, and tuition costs before making a final decision. For example, you may prefer to attend a college close to home. In contrast, you may prefer to attend school in another state or to study abroad. You must understand the full scope of your costs when selecting a school, including tuition fees, housing, and living expenses.

To gain admission into many colleges and universities, you must demonstrate your academic capabilities through standardized college entrance examinations such as the SAT or ACT. To prepare for these tests, you should familiarize yourself with the material tested on these exams and practice taking mock tests so you can answer all questions accurately when completing the tests. Additionally, building strong study habits before applying for college can significantly increase success when attending classes.

Once accepted into a college or university, you must understand financial assistance (aid) options to ensure your college costs remain manageable throughout your studies. Financial assistance can come in the form of scholarships or grants, which do not need repayment after graduation but are need-based instead of merit-based, or loans that require repayment after graduation but have relatively low-interest rates compared to other types of loans. Similarly, funding sources like institutional work-study programs may help cover some educational costs.

As a college student, you will also need to develop a budget plan to help manage your expenses in school and after graduation. When creating this budget plan, you need to evaluate all your potential income sources (e.g., part-time jobs, income from Internet sales, etc.) against your expected expenses (e.g., textbooks, housing expenses, food, etc.) to figure out how much money you have left after paying bills each month. This initial budget plan is flexible and can be adjusted over time to align with your lifestyle and goals better.

College readiness pre-work is only the first step in preparing to navigate college and life. Additional work is needed to ensure you are emotionally prepared, have a strong sense of identity, understand how you learn and your preferred methods to learn, maintain your motivation, understand the services and resources available to you in college, successfully navigate personal and professional relationships, plan for managing your time, harness your unique experiences to find your leadership voice, develop necessary professional documents to prepare you for career success, and consistently and meaningfully engage in self-care. These topics will be covered in *A.C.E.S. for Students: Strategies for Success in the First Year of College & Beyond.*

Introduction to the A.C.E.S. Framework™

I developed the A.C.E.S. Framework™ over my 30-year career as an undergraduate, trade school, graduate, doctoral, law school, and continuing education student, as well as navigating my professional career as an entry-level employee, university staff member, tenure-track/tenured university professor, attorney, and entrepreneur. Before developing the A.C.E.S. Framework™, I often found myself overwhelmed, with inconsistent results, a lack of purpose, and low motivation. However, after developing and implementing the A.C.E.S. Framework™, not only did I find a repeatable method that allowed me to map out my goals, but I also found strategies to help me to understand myself better, to know how I best study, work, and communicate, and to identify resources and skills that I possessed and needed to help me reach my goals. I wish to share the A.C.E.S. Framework™ with you and students worldwide to help you each achieve your goals.

The A.C.E.S. Framework™ is a principal tenet that I have developed and used to assist me in navigating college and life for more than 30 years. I have also used these principles in my teaching practices for more than 17 years to help students and educators lead empowered, productive lives by synthesizing their goals, coalescing their resources, igniting their passions, and sharpening their skill sets. The A.C.E.S. Framework™ teaches techniques for being:

- **Achievement-driven**—Maintaining a focus on your goals and desired outcomes.

- **Capacity-informed**—Continuously assessing and evaluating the resources you have and need to assist you in meeting your goals and desired outcomes.
- **Enthusiasm-oriented**—Ensuring your goals align with your personal and professional interests and motivations and support continued interest in development and growth.
- **Skill-building-focused**—Continuously assessing and evaluating the skills you have and need to assist you in meeting your goals and desired outcomes.

A.C.E.S. for Students is the definitive guide to give college students the preparation they need for college success. Each chapter of this book uses the A.C.E.S. Framework™ to help students develop the skills, habits, and systems required to be successful in college and after graduation. The book covers vital issues like professors' expectations, available resources, and the challenges of college life, to name a few. The early chapters focus on mindset. Next, the book covers college challenges and how to address them. Finally, the book discusses the personal skill-building necessary for success in the college environment and beyond.

As you read the book, each chapter concludes with an "Implement your A.C.E.S.™" section. These sections include several questions designed to help you develop a personal understanding of yourself and your goals, motivations, and resources. Be sure to contemplate each question and write comprehensive responses. Some questions may require you to complete research about yourself or your goals, motivations, or resources. If so, conduct thorough research, so you have the best, detailed information possible. After thoroughly completing all 13 "Implement your A.C.E.S.™ sections, you should have a comprehensive understanding of the following:

1. Your emotional intelligence,
2. Your self-identity,
3. Your motivations, preferred learning styles, and learning methods,
4. The strategies you will use to navigate college resources,
5. Your personal and professional relationship expectations,
6. The basic techniques you will use for college readiness,
7. Your time and task management strategies,
8. A plan describing how you will maximize your faculty and staff knowledge,
9. Your career search approach,
10. Your plan for finding your leadership voice, and
11. The systems you will use to maintain your mental hygiene and self-care.

Before you continue reading, answer the following questions and write your Ultimate A.C.E.S.™.

THE ULTIMATE A.C.E.S.™

1. **Achievement-driven**—What is your life goal?

2. **Capacity-informed**—What resources do you have, and what resources do you need to meet this goal?
3. **Enthusiasm-oriented**—What motivates you to reach this goal?
4. **Skill-building-focused**—What current skills do you have to assist in meeting this goal, what skills do you need to acquire to meet this goal, *and* what tasks, education, work, volunteer, or professional development opportunities are available to help you build skills required to help you complete this goal?

As you complete each "Implement your A.C.E.S.™" activity in the chapters, you should keep this ultimate A.C.E.S.™ in mind.

Part 1: Mindset
Believe in Yourself

Chapter 1
Emotional Intelligence
Emotions: Chemical Mess or Something You
Can Control?

"Being sure you can handle all the things coming your way is important. I really had to look at myself before deciding to go to college."
~ Matt C., college senior

According to *Vantage Circle* contributor Braja Deepon Roy, more than half of job performance comes from how people handle their emotions, three-quarters of Fortune 500 companies utilize emotional intelligence workshops as professional development opportunities, and people who exhibit emotional intelligence earn an average of $29,000 more than people who do not show emotional intelligence. As a college student, you must constantly monitor your emotions and evaluate how your actions impact others, regularly find opportunities to assess your skills, and maintain a mindset that recognizes you can continuously develop your skills and increase your personal and professional chances.

Emotional Intelligence, Growth Mindset, and Intercultural Competence

Figure 1: Aspects of Emotional Intelligence

Determining how you identify, manage, understand, and use your emotions—emotional intelligence—is essential to everyone. Managing your emotions is not a one-time fix; it is a lifelong process. This level of self-awareness can assist you in navigating personal and professional relationships and help you understand the impact you and your behaviors have on other people (see Figure 1).

Managing emotional intelligence requires you to manage and channel your emotions effectively. You have personal characteristics, attributes, beliefs, ideologies, and experiences that have shaped how you see and interact with people. Because of this, you approach interactions and relationships uniquely, using the knowledge you have gained as a roadmap to assist you in navigating various interactions.

A well-grounded level of self-awareness can help you identify your strengths and areas for improvement, understand your emotions and how you process and express the things you experience, and gauge how you impact others. When you successfully navigate your emotional intelligence, you know how your actions affect yourself and others. You simultaneously manage your emotions and interactions with others through empathy, organizational awareness, motivation, and emotional self-control (see Figure 1).

Competencies that a person practicing emotional intelligence may have are:

- self-awareness,
- achievement orientation,
- positive outlook,
- emotional self-control,
- adaptability,
- empathy,
- organizational awareness,
- coachability,
- conflict management,
- influence,
- inspirational leadership, and

- teamwork.

Those who have low levels of emotional intelligence may have a more difficult time regulating their emotions, interacting with people, and expressing their needs.

Self-awareness, self-regulation, and motivation are critical elements of emotional intelligence that you can develop during college. Self-awareness requires understanding one's values, goals, and limitations. (This topic is discussed in more detail in Chapter 2.) In contrast, self-regulation is managing emotions effectively in various contexts. Motivation means having a sense of purpose and direction in life, which leads to taking the initiative and making progress toward meaningful goals. Developing these skills will help prepare you for life after college as you transition into adulthood. As a college student practicing principles of emotional intelligence, you are setting yourself up for success as you enter the workforce or pursue further education. By building emotional intelligence early, you will have the tools necessary to reach your full potential later in life.

You may also benefit from consistent personal development and continuous improvement. Allocating time for personal development during college is essential for future success. By setting aside time to reflect on your achievement goals, resource capacity, enthusiasm for what you are doing, and skill (i.e., your A.C.E.S.™), you can find balance within your lives and take ownership of your development. With this knowledge, you can create meaningful relations with those around you and build on your current skills to succeed in college and after graduation.

When you focus on your personal, educational, and professional continuous improvement, you are more likely to be achievement-oriented and demonstrate greater resilience when faced with obstacles or failure. Likewise, you are more adaptable to new situations, ideas, topics, and tasks. Adopting this growth mindset gives you the confidence to explore new areas despite fearing failure. A study by Levine and colleagues found that students with a growth mindset had more ability to adapt to challenging tasks and eventually reach success.

A growth mindset can also assist you in preparing to be an adult. As a college student, you can prepare for the workforce by developing teamwork skills, gaining intercultural competence, and cultivating a strong work ethic. Teamwork is essential in the workplace. It allows employees to pool their collective talents and abilities to create something more beneficial than any individual could accomplish. Developing teamwork skills involves understanding team dynamics, learning how to collaborate effectively with others, and resolving conflicts that may arise.

Intercultural competence is also vital for employees entering the workforce and being able to understand different cultures and traditions, as well as displaying respect for them. As a college student, you can gain this skill by enrolling in global studies, cultural studies, or diversity studies courses, volunteering with intercultural agencies, attending intercultural events, or studying abroad to get hands-on experience.

Finally, having a solid work ethic prepares you for success in the workforce. When you demonstrate a strong work ethic, you monitor your approach to your appearance, attendance, attitude, character, communication, cooperation, relationships, organizational skills, productivity, respect, and teamwork in your personal and professional environments. In practice, this means showing up on time, being prepared to work with a pleasing disposition, and being reliable and accountable for tasks assigned.

Conclusion

As a college student, you must consistently manage your emotions and assess how your actions impact others, continuously seek opportunities to evaluate your skills, and maintain a growth mindset to have a substantial advantage over those without these skills when applying for jobs. You can prepare to join the workforce with teamwork skills, intercultural competence, and a strong work ethic.

Activate Your A.C.E.S.

Write short phrases on the lines provided. Use the Definition Box to help you.

1. Achievement-driven. What is your life goal?
   a. Describe your emotional intelligence goals.

> **Emotional Intelligence**—the ability to identify and manage one's own emotions, as well as the emotions of others
> https://www.psychologytoday.com/us/basics/emotional-intelligence
> **Intercultural skills**—techniques or behaviors that allow a person to function effectively across cultures
> https://www.monash.edu/arts/monash-intercultural-lab/about-the-monash-intercultural-lab/what-is-intercultural-competence

   _____
   _____
   _____
   _____
   _____
   _____
   _____
   _____
   _____
   _____

   b. List your requirements to interact with your family, friends, co-workers, and so on.

   _____
   _____
   _____
   _____

_____
_____
_____
_____
_____

    c. Describe the types of relationships you want to have with each group.

_____
_____
_____
_____
_____
_____

2. Capacity-informed. What resources do you have or need to get?
    a. List your personal strengths and areas for improvement that will assist you in meeting those goals.

_____
_____
_____

_____

_____

_____

_____

_____

_____

_____

3. **E**nthusiasm-oriented. What motivates you?
    a. List the things that motivate you to continue building your emotional intelligence.

_____

_____

_____

_____

_____

_____

_____

_____

4. **S**kill-building-focused. What current skills do you have? What skills do you need to gain?
    a. List the ways you could develop additional intercultural skills.

_____
_____
_____
_____
_____
_____
_____
_____
_____

b. List the resources you currently use to
   build your emotional intelligence.

_____
_____
_____
_____
_____
_____
_____
_____

c. List the help you need to develop your
   emotional intelligence but do not have.

_____
_____

_____

_____

_____

_____

_____

_____

_____

_____

d. Create an action plan to get access to the resources you need to build your emotional intelligence.

_____

_____

_____

_____

_____

_____

_____

_____

The A.C.E.S. Framework™ Check-In

Now that you know more about emotional intelligence and have deepened your understanding of this topic, take what you learned and find out how it applies to your life.

Be sure to explore the related topics and resources on https://tracycrumpenterprisesllc.com/media-press.

There, you will find a wealth of information on emotional intelligence, so take your time to brush up on what you have learned here and expand your knowledge.

In addition, be sure to stop by our social media pages and let us know what your three takeaways from this chapter were. Relating the material to your unique experience is one of the best ways to get started on your path to success.

TheACESFramework

@ACESFramework

www.linkedin.com/in/tracygcrump

Chapter 2
Find Your Self-Identity
Wait a Minute, Who Are You Again?

> "I had no idea who I was and am
> happy to know now."
> ~ Shell S., college sophomore

*F*orbes contributor Heather Cherry notes having a solid sense of self-identity supports mental and physical health and helps to minimize self-doubt and uncertainty. Developing self-identity encompasses examining your moral values, belief system, personality traits, abilities, motivations, and likes and dislikes. Understanding these unique characteristics sets the foundation for purposeful living and developing healthy relationships.

Self-Identity

Attending college presents a unique opportunity for self-exploration and growth. This transition means you become responsible for navigating your life and daily routines. To accomplish this task, you must begin the process of understanding who you are, what you like and dislike, and your strengths and areas for growth. As a college student, you face a transitional point when you are no longer solely guided by parents and guardians and are instead your primary caregiver and caretaker.

Each person develops their self-identity, self-concept, or self-awareness by understanding that they exist as a unique individual separate from others (i.e., the existential self) and as part of a larger society (i.e., the categorical self) with unique attributes, characteristics, and demographics (see Figure 2). As you grow and learn, you will begin to recognize and assess your different traits compared to others. You will also start forming and evaluating your self-image (i.e., how you see yourself), self-esteem (i.e., the value you place on yourself), and ideal self (i.e., the type of person you aspire to be). At the same time, you will begin building your foundational understanding of your social identity—your personal or internal identity (i.e., your traits) and the people, places, or things you identify with (i.e., community or cultural groups) and categorizing, identifying with, and socially comparing yourself to others.

It would help if you learned what you like and dislike (i.e., who you are) and what you value. Knowing who you are and what you value will give you the skills needed to navigate interactions with others, whether positive or negative. For example, suppose someone labels you lazy because you were asleep and not available to spend time with them at 2 PM; however, you knew the reason you were asleep was because you worked an 11 PM – 7:30 AM shift and went straight from work to a 9 AM – 12 PM class. In this instance, you can identify your goals to be successful in school and at work as priorities. In that case, you can process the information by identifying what is important to you, compare it to what you know about yourself, and develop your own conclusion about yourself. With this knowledge, you are less likely to take another person's opinion about you as the correct definition of who you are because you are the expert on yourself. You also will not rely on external praise to define who you are. Moreover, you will be able to think about and critically evaluate each interaction you have.

Figure 2: Components of Self-Identity

As a college student, you must be proactive and write a list detailing the things that are important to you personally and professionally. This initial list, and subsequent versions of the list, will not be exhaustive or static. The list will change with each iteration. However, getting the list started and revising it as your feelings or life circumstances change is crucial. Areas that may be important to consider are:

- Your family relationships,
- Your social relationships,
- Your professional relationships,
- Your personality traits,
- Your strengths and areas for improvement,
- Your culture(s),
- Your experiences and aspirations,
- How you see yourself,
- How you believe others see you,
- Your physical appearance and characteristics, and
- Your interests.

Being proactive in identifying where you are and where you desire to be will form a solid foundation for you to begin assessing the resources you have and those you need to assist you in meeting your goals. The time when you attend college can be a time of tremendous growth and change. It is common for you to find yourself undertaking the process of discovering your identity and creating new relationships inside and outside the classroom. This time can be a challenging period leading up to graduation as you decide on your career path, financial stability, familial or personal relationships, and overall personal and professional goals.

You can begin to explore your self-identity development in school by determining if clubs, organizations, or initiatives interest you on your college campus. Another helpful resource to assist you in navigating self-exploration is access to mentors and role models who can share your insights on navigating educational and life pursuits. (Chapter 12 covers mentorship in more detail.)

The time when you are in college can present internal and external pressures. It would help if you considered your mental, spiritual/communal well-being, and physical health. Personal development during this time is crucial to success after college because the process of developing self-identity also cultivates the skills needed to be resilient and helps you develop coping mechanisms such as problem-solving skills or emotional intelligence, which enables you to navigate difficult moments that come with life's challenges.

Motivation is a critical element of classroom success. You can be motivated to perform better in your classes by setting specific and achievable goals. Setting short-term and long-term goals is essential, as this allows you to track your progress over time. As a college student, you should reward yourself for reaching milestones, such as completing assignments or getting good test grades, to help you stay motivated. It also reinforces positive behaviors and encourages you to strive toward academic goals. Connect with peers or colleagues pursuing the same degree or taking similar courses and work together to motivate each other throughout the semester. Doing so will create a sense of community that can provide additional motivation when you feel you need it most.

Conclusion

Taking time to understand yourself and making conscious decisions about your personal and social environment will allow you to become more aware of who you are and what you need to achieve a rewarding life after graduation. Further, reflecting on the present moment and creating meaningful connections with those around you will help set the stage for your future success. With the proper guidance, commitment, and resources, you can use your college time to find your purpose and your identity.

Activate Your A.C.E.S.

Write short phrases on the lines provided. Use the Definition Box to help you.

1. Achievement-driven.
   What is your life goal?
   a. Describe your self-identity goals.

   _____

   _____

Self-identity—A person's understanding of who they are based on their values, experiences, and relationships.
https://www.psychologytoday.com/us/basics/identity

_____

_____

_____

_____

_____

_____

b. Describe your moral values, beliefs, personality traits, abilities, motivations, and likes and dislikes.

_____

_____

_____

_____

_____

_____

_____

_____

2. Capacity-informed. What resources do you have or need to get?

   a. Explain how you respond to specific stimuli.

_____

_____

_____

_____

_____

_____

_____
_____
_____

3. Enthusiasm-oriented. What motivates you?
    a. Describe the things that are important to you in the following areas:
    b. your family relationships
    c. your social relationships
    d. your professional relationships
    e. your personality traits
    f. your strengths and areas for improvement
    g. your culture(s)
    h. your experiences and aspirations
    i. how you see yourself
    j. how you believe others see you
    k. your physical appearance and characteristics
    l. your interests

_____
_____
_____
_____
_____
_____
_____
_____
_____

4. **S**kill-building-focused. What current skills do you have? What skills do you need to gain?
   a. List the resources you currently use build your self-identity.

   _____

   _____

   _____

   _____

   _____

   _____

   _____

   _____

   b. List the help you need to develop your self-identity but do not have.

   _____

   _____

   _____

   _____

   _____

   _____

   _____

   _____

c. Create an action plan to access resources to develop your self-identity.

_____
_____
_____
_____
_____
_____
_____
_____
_____
_____

The A.C.E.S. Framework™ Check-In

Now that you know more about your self-identity and have deepened your understanding of this topic, take what you learned and find out how it applies to your life.

Be sure to explore the related topics and resources on https://tracycrumpenterprisesllc.com/media-press.

There, you will find a wealth of information on self-identity, so take your time to brush up on what you have learned here and expand your knowledge.

In addition, be sure to stop by our social media pages and let us know what your three takeaways from this chapter were. Relating the material to your unique experience is one of the best ways to get started on your path to success.

TheACESFramework

@ACESFramework

www.linkedin.com/in/tracygcrump

Chapter 3
Motivation
Crushing Your Goals when it's Hard to Leave the Bed

> "Knowing my 'why' has helped me stay on track."
> ~ Phil B., college junior

Julien S. Bureau and colleagues' recent research found clarity about why you want to achieve a goal (i.e., your motivation), and implementing a system to meet your goals increases the quality of a learning experience and the likelihood of achieving an objective. Staying motivated in college is vital to college success. Identifying the reasons you enrolled in college and the reasons you are pursuing the degree you are seeking can assist you in developing an action plan with measurable milestones to ensure your success. You can increase your chances of remaining motivated by rewarding your accomplishments and communicating with peers, advisors, or mentors throughout your college experience. Having a personal mission statement as a guiding light helps to keep you on track toward meeting your goals.

Developing Motivation for the Long Haul

Staying engaged and motivated is critical to having a positive college experience. Motivations are why people behave in specific ways. Different things inspire people, and if you plan to be successful in college, you need to find out what will motivate you to do your best personally, academically, and professionally. Specifically, identifying what your goal is and why you want to reach that goal can assist you as you are placing the resources you have and those you need to accomplish your objective.

Likewise, creating a clear vision and plan to attain your goal allows you to identify milestones toward reaching your goal and offers a roadmap and checklist to illustrate what you have accomplished, your future path, and how far you need to go to achieve your objective. This also goes a long way toward helping you to organize your tasks and resources into manageable undertakings. Further, this will allow you to visualize your progress more concretely toward your goal and to identify areas for improvement, strengths, successes, and challenges.

One of the most effective ways to increase motivation is to focus on intrinsic motivation. Intrinsic motivation involves an individual's internal drive or desire to engage in a particular behavior or activity. It can be encouraged by creating a meaningful environment that allows individuals to strive for self-determination, autonomy, and a sense of accomplishment.

Increasing career motivation is an integral part of the college experience. You can increase your career motivation by using several strategies and activities to help you make the most of your college years. One fundamental approach for motivation is to focus on goal-setting and achievement. By setting realistic goals that are achievable in a college environment, you can make strides toward reaching your desired career outcomes. Additionally, creating a timeline or schedule for completing tasks related to achieving these goals can help you stay motivated and focused on your results.

Another way to increase your career motivation is to take advantage of available resources. Colleges typically offer workshops, mentorships, internships, job fairs, and other opportunities that provide you with valuable insights into different career paths. These resources can offer you the knowledge and skills necessary to make informed decisions about your time in college and your future career. Chapters 11 and 12 will cover these resources in more detail.

As a college student, you should prioritize activities likely to increase your motivation and provide greater job satisfaction. Internships, volunteer work, and extracurriculars related to a desired field of study can help you develop skills while also gaining experience you can use to build a career after graduation. Investing in experiences like these is essential in increasing motivation and maintaining positive momentum while in college.

Developing a personal mission statement will also increase your motivation, goal-setting, and achievement. A personal mission statement explains who you are and why you do what you do. You can use reflective writing to develop your mission statement. Reflective writing requires you to think critically about your experiences and how they have impacted you and how you view the world. Taking advantage of available resources and investing in college experiences will help you better understand your experiences and be more motivated throughout college and beyond.

Conclusion

Your motivation explains your "why" for your actions, what you say, and what you believe. Better understanding your motivation is an active pursuit that includes identifying your goals and being able to measure when you achieve milestones toward reaching them. Goal-setting requires you to develop a clear plan detailing the steps you need to take to reach your goals, identify the intrinsic rewards that are important to you, monitor progress toward your goals by mapping out the incremental steps it will take you to reach your destination, and reward yourself as you surpass each milestone.

Additionally, after reaching milestones, you can challenge yourself by setting new goals, engaging an accountability partner or mentor, identifying possible challenges beforehand, and identifying resources that will help you address challenges if they arise (i.e., making an obstacle plan). Be sure to show yourself some grace by recognizing everyone makes mistakes. If you make a mistake, you can learn from it because it presents an opportunity for growth.

Be sure to consistently revisit your goal's "why" as you develop and revise your mission statement. Also, engage in personal and professional development activities to sharpen your skills to reach and exceed your goals and create your mission statement. As such, it is crucial to identify not only why you are motivated in the present but also what will keep you motivated into the future.

Activate Your A.C.E.S.

Write short phrases on the lines provided. Use the Definition Box to help you.

> **Motivation**—the internal drive that desires change.
> https://positivepsychology.com/what-is-motivation/

1. Achievement-driven. What is your life goal?
    a. Describe your goal for staying motivated.

    _____

    _____

    _____

    _____

    _____

    _____

    _____

    _____

_____

_____

b. Write your mission statement.

_____

_____

_____

_____

_____

_____

_____

_____

_____

2. Capacity-informed. What resources do you have or need to get?
   a. Explain what intrinsically motivates you (i.e., non-monetary things that make you feel like you want to do or be part of something).

_____

_____

_____

_____

_____

_____

_____
_____
_____

3. **E**nthusiasm-oriented. What motivates you?
   a. List the things that motivate you for each goal above.

   _____
   _____
   _____
   _____
   _____
   _____
   _____
   _____
   _____

   b. List the rewards you would consider for yourself as you reach each milestone.

   _____
   _____
   _____
   _____
   _____

_____
_____
_____
_____
_____

4. <u>S</u>kill-building-focused. What current skills do you have? What skills do you need to gain?
    a. List the resources you currently have to maintain your motivation.

    _____
    _____
    _____
    _____
    _____
    _____
    _____
    _____

    b. List the resources you need to build your motivation but do not have.

    _____
    _____
    _____
    _____

_____
_____
_____
_____
_____

c. Create an action plan to get access to the necessary resources to build your motivation.

_____
_____
_____
_____
_____
_____
_____
_____
_____

The A.C.E.S. Framework™ Check-In

Now that you know more about motivation and have deepened your understanding of this topic, take what you learned and find out how it applies to your life.

Be sure to explore the related topics and resources on https://tracycrumpenterprisesllc.com/media-press.

There, you will find a wealth of information on motivation, so take your time to brush up on what you have learned here and expand your knowledge.

In addition, be sure to stop by our social media pages and let us know what your three takeaways from this chapter were. Relating the material to your unique experience is one of the best ways to get started on your path to success.

TheACESFramework

@ACESFramework

www.linkedin.com/in/tracygcrump

Part 2: Practical Skills for College Success
Prepare Yourself

Chapter 4
Understand Your Learning Styles, Note-Taking Methods, and Learning Methods
How Learning Can Be Fun (I Know, I Know, You Never Thought Those Two Would Go Together)

"Knowing the different ways I learn is helpful in class and when I do my homework."
~ Bella Q.,
college senior

According to Kulkarni and colleagues, many professors use the learning style approach when preparing their lesson plans. Historically, there is a consensus in education that people prefer to have certain information presented to them in specific ways, and they use various methods to learn and retain information. Understanding your preferred methods for accessing and continuously learning information is vital in college and throughout your life. Although you may not like using the same techniques to consume information, depending on the subject, if you know which methods you prefer, you can better prepare yourself and identify the resources you need to support your success.

Learning Styles

People prefer to receive information in different ways. Some people learn and retain information better if they read it, others prefer the information to be spoken, and still, others prefer information to be presented in pictures, images, graphs, or infographics. Several well-recognized learning styles are visual, aural, verbal, physical, logical, social, and solitary learning styles.

Visual learners prefer using pictures, images, and spatial understanding when accessing and retaining information. These learners may benefit from making outlines, using flashcards, creating graphs and charts, accessing handouts that concisely explain concepts and material, or mapping out information visually using symbols or pictures.

Aural learners respond to the use of sound or music to grasp information. These learners may incorporate vignettes or short videos that briefly explain information, use dictation software and hardware to record and review material, read material aloud, and discuss concepts with others.

Verbal learners may prefer using words in speech and writing to understand information. These learners may benefit from using acronyms or mnemonic devices and mirroring or parroting information.

Physical or kinesthetic learners may prefer using their bodies, hands, and sense of touch to synthesize information. Physical learners may benefit from tactile experiences and desire to engage in a line-by-line information assessment to work through challenges.

Logical or mathematical learners may benefit from using logic, reasoning, and systems to make sense of information. Methods such as pattern recognition exercises, understanding connections, and adopting classification strategies help this learner understand and remember information.

Social or interpersonal learners may prefer to learn in groups or with other people. Social learners may benefit from verbal and non-verbal learning environments that allow them to articulate concerns, ask questions, and compare ideas in one-on-one or group settings.

Solitary or intrapersonal learners may prefer to work alone and use self-study. Solitary learners may benefit from understanding self-reflection strategies that allow them to assess strengths and weaknesses and receive guidance on practices to improve. They may also benefit from understanding their study environment's role in their productivity (i.e., they may prefer to study (and best perform) in quiet, remote locations).

While recognizing these learning styles, we must note that there are other learning styles. Most people do not prefer one learning style to access and retain all information. Sometimes, a person may like reading information on one subject and seeing information depicted as an infographic on another topic. Once you understand your learning styles for each subject, you may tailor your note-taking and learning methods to fit your needs best. Additionally, you may consider developing a plan to manage how you use your study time. One method you may consider is the Pomodoro Technique.

Task-Management Technique: The Pomodoro Technique

Managing the time you allocate toward completing your assignments is an important task. It would help if you thought critically about the time you will need to finish tasks to the best of your ability. If you do not, you often find yourself rushed to complete tasks without enough time to finish or you submit work that does not best represent you or your capabilities. One task management technique developed by Francesco Cirillo in the 1980s may assist in prioritizing the task and increasing student focus.

The Pomodoro technique divides work into small increments (25 minutes) called "Pomodoros." Each increment is separated with a short break (five minutes) until the task is finished. To begin a Pomodoro, you set a 25-minute timer. During each Pomodoro, you focus on completing a task without distraction. When the timer rings, you take a five-minute break. After the break, you return to the task and complete the same steps outlined above until finished. If the task takes longer than four Pomodoros, you can take longer breaks of 15 to 30 minutes between every four Pomodoro intervals.

This strategy can be beneficial for those who have difficulty staying motivated and help avoid procrastination. By breaking up long study sessions into smaller chunks and taking regular breaks, you can ensure that you produce your best work efficiently. Additionally, it can help eliminate the feeling of being overwhelmed and help you stay organized throughout your studies.

Note-Taking Methods

Note-taking is an integral part of the college classroom experience. It is good practice to take notes in each class and review them before the next class. You can use several methods to take notes. Your chosen method will depend on your preferred learning style(s) for the course material and discipline. You may use one note-taking form for one course and another technique for a different course. Remember, whichever way you choose, ensure that it is a comfortable and logical method for you and that it will assist you in retaining, recalling, and studying the material later.

Figure 3: The Charting Method

WHAT?	EATING	EXERCISING	SLEEPING
ADVANTAGE	Fuels the body	Builds stamina and muscle	Reenergizes body
DISADVANTAGE	Must know how to cook	Need time to consistently do it	Can't get enough
WHEN APPROPRIATE	Always	Always	Always

The Charting Method

This method breaks information into categories like a spreadsheet (see Figure 3). It requires you to create columns by drawing vertical lines on lined notebook paper. You will label each column with appropriate headings in a table according to the topics discussed. As the lecture proceeds, you write the information in words, phrases, and main ideas into the appropriate columns or rows. This technique presents information in an easy-to-read format, but it is not the best technique if there is a lot of information or if you do not know the topics covered before the lecture.

The Charting Method has strengths and weaknesses. The biggest strength of charting note-taking is its ability to provide an organized overview of the material. It enables you to quickly review topics, key ideas, and associations between the various elements of a subject. Charting can also be used to compare two topics, helping you understand their relationship. By visually presenting information, charting makes it easier for you to remember and recall this material later when needed. However, despite its advantages, there are some limitations associated with charting. For example, it may be challenging to distinguish between the various elements within a chart since each component can appear similar in size and shape. Additionally, because the information typically appears in neat rows and columns, making quick associations or drawing meaningful conclusions from your notes could be challenging without thoroughly reviewing the material. Lastly, it may be challenging to access specific notes quickly if you have not familiarized yourself with the chart format.

Figure 4: The Cornell Method

Topic:	Name:
Source:	Class:
	Date:

Cues/Keywords (questions you have)	Notes (facts from class session)

Summary (your notes in your words)

The Cornell Method

Authors Walter Pauk and Ross J. Q. Owens popularized taking notes by dividing a page into three sections labeled "notes," "cues," and "summary" (see Figure 4). During the lecture (or when reviewing an online lecture), write the facts in the "notes" section. Do not write the lecture word-for-word. Instead, capture the gist of what is said and the necessary details that help you understand the material. As questions arise, write them down in the "cues" section and answer them later. It would help if you wrote any insights or comments about the material covered. Generally, the "cues" section is used after class is over to help synthesize material; however, the "cues" and "notes" sections can be used simultaneously. After class, while reviewing your notes, write your understanding of the material in the "summary" section.

You should write this information as if you were explaining the material to another person new to the topic.

The Cornell Method has strengths and weaknesses. One of the significant strengths of this method is its simplicity. It is easy to understand and can be adapted differently depending on your preferences. It also facilitates active learning by encouraging you to interact with the material you are studying and think critically about it. The main downside of this method is that it can be time-consuming. You must read through notes, jot down cue words, and summarize content in your own words, which can take a lot of effort and energy. Additionally, you may miss important details and ideas if you are not a detailed note-taker.

Figure 5: The Outline Method

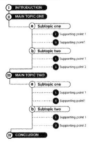

The Outline Method
When using this method, the lecture notes are organized hierarchically and identify the relationship between main

details and sub-details (see Figure 5). You create the list by identifying each main point and then presenting the sub-topics of a central point below the main point while indenting to the next level. As the lecture progresses, you fill in facts and details in your respective main points or sub-detail sections.

The outline method has strengths and weaknesses. The main strength of the outline method is that it can help study and summarize material quickly and create a comprehensive overview of a topic. However, the outline note-taking method also has some drawbacks. One of the main issues is that it can be challenging to capture all the details and nuances of a topic when creating an outline. This can lead to a need for more understanding or context around certain concepts. Additionally, outlines may only sometimes provide enough structure for further analysis and discussion because it may require more work to connect the main points in a meaningful way.

Figure 6: The Mind-Map Method

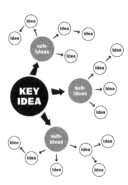

Mind-Map Method

Mind-mapped notes create an image of concepts and relationships using visuals, abstractions, and associations (see Figure 6). Start by writing a list of key terms from your lecture. Next, define each of the main terms. Plot the main topics on the page with room between each. Ask yourself how each of the critical terms relate to each other (i.e., are they similar or different, is there a cause-and-effect relationship, are they part of a larger whole, etc.). Mark the relationships by writing between the terms to depict the relationships visually. Make your mind map easy to show how your ideas flow and how you understand the thought process (color code or highlight to indicate changes or different functions).

The mind-map method has strengths and weaknesses. One of the main advantages of mind maps is that they are highly visual. Mind-mapping enables learners to capture details in an organized and easily accessible way, making it easier to recall and consolidate information. Mind maps also require less time and effort to review and process. Furthermore, mind maps provide an effective way of organizing complex data in a logical and easily understandable manner. By using arrows, tables, and other visuals, it is possible to create a hierarchy of ideas that allows for more straightforward navigation through complex topics or systems. However, there are also some drawbacks associated with the mind-mapping method. For example, the diagrams become too extensive or detailed. In that case, reading and understanding the information presented in them can be challenging.

Additionally, this type of note-taking is time-consuming. Creating an effective diagram requires a great deal of focus and concentration. Furthermore, mind maps may be less efficient for shorter notes or memorizing facts, as other methods may better suit these tasks.

Figure 7: The Sentence Method

Date Today **Topic** Today's topic

1. I need to show up for every class.

2. I need to take notes in every class.

3. I need to review my notes for every class.

4. I need to drink water every day.

5. I need to exercise.

6. I need to eat well.

7. I need to sleep well.

8. I am going to CRUSH college!

The Sentence Method

Write down everything the instructor says and use a separate line for each statement, thought, or point (see Figure 7). You may want to use bullet points or numbers to separate each statement, thought, or point visually. If you abbreviate or use shorthand, document what the abbreviations mean. You will need to review your notes to find the key points and better understand the lecture's essential elements.

The Sentence Method has strengths and weaknesses. The primary advantage of this approach is that it allows you to capture information quickly in an organized manner. The sentences can be easily referenced and recalled during exams or while writing papers. Additionally, since the notes are more concise than traditional methods, there is less chance of forgetting important information. However, there are also some potential drawbacks to using the sentence method of note-taking. For example, it requires more discipline and focuses on being effective. Additionally, since the notes are more condensed, you may miss important details or contexts that can be important during exams or presentations.

Figure 8: The Zettelkasten Method

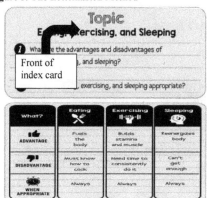

The Zettelkasten Method
The Zettelkasten Method allows you to organize your notes systematically and to make connections between concepts. Take notes using one of the other types of note-taking techniques. Summarize those notes and write them

in your own words briefly on one side of an index card. Write the reference information on the other side of the index card to allow you to be able to retrieve the source later (see Figure 8). After completing your notes, go back through the index cards and add additional ideas, arguments, connections, and answers to questions you may have had about the material. Also include keywords on note cards. File your note cards in an index card box, one behind the other. As you continue to study, add relationships and connections to the note cards. File each note card in a way that will make it easy for you to retrieve the information. You may also include a "fleeting notes" section that you will follow up on later and further develop to add to your main note card section.

The Zettelkasten Method has strengths and weaknesses. The primary benefit of the Zettelkasten method is its flexibility. You can record, store, and connect the information in many ways. The Zettelkasten process allows you to access relevant material as you need it. Additionally, the method encourages creativity and critical thinking by helping you to generate new ideas and make connections between different topics. The Zettelkasten method also has some potential drawbacks. It relies heavily on your ability to organize information, which can be time-consuming and challenging. Furthermore, it may require a significant effort to update the system by regularly adding new information and connections.

Learning Methods

Studying, or continuous learning, occurs when you devote time and attention to reviewing course materials to acquire knowledge, synthesize information, and confirm understanding. You can use various learning methods depending on your preferred learning styles. Like note-taking, your learning method will depend on your selected learning styles for the course material and discipline. You may use one study technique for one course and another for a different course. Remember, whichever method you choose, ensure that it is a learning method that is comfortable and logical to you and will assist you in retaining and recalling information for later use.

Spaced/Distributed Practice (When You Could Study)
Use this learning method to review the material over multiple sessions at different points in time. For example, you can review lecture notes or a chapter in the textbook in the evening or the day following the lecture to reinforce learning and to better understand previously "fuzzy" concepts. You could use the topics listed on the course syllabus as a guide when preparing your day-by-day or week-by-week routine learning schedule. Each learning session should be prescheduled and only cover the previously selected topics (i.e., do not attempt to cover all the material in one session). The material covered should be a mix of new and previously learned material. Spacing out learning the material over time helps you internalize your understanding instead of just memorizing it. Additionally, spaced/distributed practice decreases the likelihood that you will cram large amounts of material into short study sessions.

Retrieval Practice and Practice Testing (How You Could Study)
This learning method is a recall-based learning technique allowing you to complete practice tests to assess your retained understanding. For example, you could remove all your course materials, use a blank sheet of paper or document, and try to recall as much information about the topic as you can. Additionally, you could complete practice tests, older versions of tests covering the same material, or create your tests. You could also create and use flashcards with questions on one side and answers on the other. By using retrieval practice, you could increase the likelihood of successfully remembering important information when you need to recall it.

Elaboration (How You Could Study)
During the lecture, reading, or note-taking process, write down questions about the material. After your session, find the answers to your questions. Next, check your understanding with your professor or someone who has mastered the topic. Subsequently, take connections between the topics you are studying in the course and note how you compare, are similar, or are dissimilar. Be as accurate as possible, and do not embellish your elaborations by adding untested, unconfirmed, or questionable information. Try to apply the material you are learning to your own experiences or the information you have received throughout your life. Continue to review, recall, and reexamine the information until you can explain the topic without using your notes.

Interleaving (How You Could Study)

Interleaving requires studying different topics in one session. Each issue is studied until you feel you confidently understand the material. While learning, you take a short break and then return to learn a different topic until you feel confident you know it. You can mix up the concepts you study or the problems you learn. Be sure not to try to explore too many topics in one session. Also, do not spend too little time on any one topic because you want to ensure you have enough time to understand the concepts.

Additionally, be sure to mix up the order in which you study the topics to allow you to identify connections between concepts. Interleaving helps to improve information retention by reviewing the information in short sessions at different times while mixing up the order of topics within the subject you are studying. This method also helps you identify similarities, differences, connections, and relationships among topics within a subject. You learn the appropriate skill to use and how to effectively employ the skill to address the issue or solve the problem.

Dual Coding (How You Could Study)
Using this learning method combines words (written representation) and images (visual representation) with learning information and connecting the word to an image and connecting concepts. You can find visuals (such as graphics, charts, or pictures) that explain concepts during the lecture, reading, or note-taking process. You then compare the visuals to the words describing the concepts and develop a statement explaining the ideas in your

words. You should check your understanding with someone who has mastered the material (i.e., your professor) and then draw or produce your own visual to explain the concept (e.g., an infographic, a timeline, or a cartoon strip, or by diagraming relationships). After repeated recall sessions, you should attempt to draw your visuals and write out explanations without using your notes.

Concrete Examples (What You Could Study)
Create a document with examples covered in your textbook(s) and other class resources, and those covered by your instructor. In your own words, write a statement explaining how the covered topic relates to each example given. Assess your understanding by explaining your information to others knowledgeable about the subject (e.g., your professor) and determine if your explanation is correct.

A Note on Using Multiple Learning Styles, Note-Taking Practices, and Learning Methods
In most cases, you will use multiple learning styles to access information. For example, you may begin by reading material, progress to watching video lectures on the same material, and ultimately move to practice the techniques learned to confirm your understanding. You will likely use multiple note-taking strategies to capture your knowledge of course material. As such, you may begin by outlining during the course lecture, then use the Cornell Method to write more detailed notes and summaries, and then engage in mind mapping to synthesize the material to explain your understanding to

your professor. Likewise, you may use multiple learning methods to ensure you understand the material. For instance, you may begin by creating concrete examples to explain concepts, then progress to completing practice tests before ultimately reviewing material over multiple sessions at different points.

Conclusion

You will likely have a unique mix of learning styles, note-taking, and learning methods. Each combination of techniques may differ from class to class and from subject to subject. Understanding your preferred methods for accessing and continuously learning information is essential in college and throughout your life. While you may not like using the same ways all the time, knowing the techniques you prefer can help you prepare to master information in college and beyond. Having this understanding can also assist you in identifying the services and resources you will need to be successful.

Activate Your A.C.E.S.

Write short phrases on the lines provided. Use the Definition Box to help you.

1. Achievement-driven. What is your life goal?
   a. Explain how you prefer to receive information for each course you plan to enroll in while attending college.

   _____
   _____
   _____

   _____
   _____
   _____
   _____
   _____
   _____

   b. Describe how you like to record information for each course you plan to enroll in while attending college.

   _____
   _____

_____
_____
_____
_____
_____
_____
_____

2. Capacity-informed. What resources do you have
   or need to get?
   a. Describe how you retain information for
      each course you plan to enroll in while
      attending college.

_____
_____
_____
_____
_____
_____
_____

3. Enthusiasm-oriented. What motivates you?
   a. Describe why you prefer to receive
      information in the way you listed above.

_____
_____
_____
_____
_____
_____
_____
_____
_____

b. Describe why you like to record information in the way you listed above.

_____
_____
_____
_____
_____
_____

4. **S**kill-building-focused. What current skills do you have? What skills do you need to gain?

a. List the resources you currently use to help you learn.

_____
_____
_____
_____
_____
_____
_____
_____
_____
_____

b. List the resources you need to help you learn but do not have.

_____
_____
_____
_____
_____
_____
_____
_____
_____
_____

c. Create an action plan to get access to the resources you need to access these resources.

_____

_____

_____

_____

_____

_____

_____

_____

_____

The A.C.E.S. Framework™ Check-In

Now that you know more about learning styles, note-taking methods, and learning methods and have deepened your understanding of this topic, take what you learned and find out how it applies to your life.

Be sure to explore the related topics and resources on https://tracycrumpenterprisesllc.com/media-press.

There, you will find a wealth of information on learning styles, note-taking methods, and learning methods, so take your time to brush up on what you have learned here and expand your knowledge.

In addition, be sure to stop by our social media pages and let us know what your three takeaways from this chapter were. Relating the material to your unique experience is one of the best ways to get started on your path to success.

TheACESFramework

@ACESFramework

www.linkedin.com/in/tracygcrump

Chapter 5
Pre-Semester Activities
Finding Out What's Available On Campus

"Knowing about my campus before I want to class was really helpful."
~ Mary C., college sophomore

Theresa Sullivan Barger of *University Business* notes that attending campus orientation sessions results in students learning about resources available on campus. Those who effectively use the help throughout their enrollment likely have a more positive college experience and higher grades. Many activities occur in the days, weeks, and months before school starts. Evaluating your educational opportunities generally means assessing whether institutions are a good fit for you and if you are a good fit for the institution. Pre-semester activities can assist you in learning about the campus, understanding the resources available, meeting the campus community, and setting up needed resources to ensure your success.

Campus Visit Days and Student Orientation
The first day of class is not the first day of school. Several important pre-semester activities play a vital role in determining if the institution is a good fit for you and if

you are a good fit for the institution. One of the first activities that you undertake is campus visit/accepted student days and new student orientation. Generally, during student orientation, you and your parents or guardians get an introduction to the institution and its academic programs, policies, student code of conduct, and student support services. You may also receive a tour of the campus and support service offices. You may have the opportunity to register for courses for the upcoming semester. You can also find out what items you will need to bring to campus with you. Be sure to download your free College Essentials Checklist from Tracy Crump Enterprises, LLC. This checklist explains:

- important places to locate on or near your campus,
- things college students should know before going to college,
- things college student should have before going to college, and
- items college students should remember to pack when going away to college.

Additionally, you may meet faculty, staff, and administrators participating in the orientation activities. You may also find out when you can take your placement tests—an examination designed to evaluate your preexisting subject understanding to determine an appropriate level to begin studying the subject. Other areas typically covered during student orientation are accessing financial aid, student housing, meal plans, setting up school accounts (email, etc.), building access restrictions, institutional transportation, public transportation, transit card availability, and access to taxis or rideshare services. Even after attending student orientation, you should devote time to learning about the institution, its culture, and where offices, classrooms, and buildings you will need are located. One way to do this is to explore the campus and talk to people there.

Deciding on Institutional Fit

When determining whether a post-secondary institution (i.e., college or university) is a good fit for you, it is crucial to consider the academic offerings, culture, and student life at the college to determine if it meets your needs and expectations. A lot of this research can be conducted when visiting a campus prior to making a decision and during campus tours or orientation. Be sure to download your free College Fit Questionnaire from Tracy Crump Enterprises, LLC. This questionnaire provides 29 questions you should consider when choosing a college.

In terms of academics, investigate courses offered by the college and departmental requirements. Make sure the school has what you are looking for academically, whether that is a specific major or an opportunity to take classes in different areas. Additionally, research your approach to learning by finding out the types of experiential learning opportunities you have, how your classes are structured, and if you offer any specialized programs that interest you.

To get an idea of culture and student life, research clubs and activities offered at the school, student populations, location, and campus atmosphere. Research student reviews online to understand how current students and alums perceive the school. Also, consider what extracurricular activities you would like to participate in, such as sports or theater productions, and find out if the institution has them available.

You may also consider contacting faculty members in your major or staff members at the institution and asking about your research opportunities or career services available on campus. Likewise, you should consider requesting to audit (sit in on) a class session in your perspective major to get a sense of how classes progress, student engagement, and professors' expectations. Another way to get a better impression of a college or university is to visit their website and attend their informational events – both virtual and in-person.

Commuter Students
Many college students do not live on campus and must commute to attend classes. College commuter students face a unique challenge: staying involved despite limited access to resources. Fortunately, several strategies can help make the most of your college experience if you are a commuter student. One of the most effective methods for promoting involvement is to actively search out organizations and extracurricular activities that cater to commuter students' interests.

Clubs or student groups focused on engaging commuter students offer an ideal opportunity for commuters to connect with others who share similar experiences. Additionally, many colleges provide carpooling or ridesharing services specifically designed for commuter students, reducing transportation costs while providing an outlet for meeting new people. Similarly, some schools have special events such as "commuter lunches" or "commuter teas" to help encourage socialization and foster community.

Another approach for commuters is to explore campus opportunities. Commuter students can serve in many campus-wide roles, from student government positions to volunteer projects. By participating, commuters can have an active voice in shaping their college experience and make a difference in the lives of fellow students. Campus participation often provides a valuable experience that will prove advantageous after graduation.

Commuter students could also take advantage of opportunities to engage with the local community. Many colleges offer access to nearby resources such as libraries, museums, or theaters at a reduced or no cost, giving commuters easy access to cultural enrichment opportunities. Furthermore, reaching out to local businesses can result in internships or job opportunities, enabling commuter students to gain practical experience, generate extra income, and network.

A Note on Transferring
In some cases, students may believe an institution is a good fit for them but find out the institution is not right for them after experiencing the campus culture or beginning classes. In these cases, students may contemplate

transferring. When deciding to transfer, you should consider several important factors. These include the potential financial implications of transferring, as well as any academic risks that may be associated with the process. Sometimes, you may need to take extra steps to secure financial aid at another institution. Sometimes, the course credits you earned at your first institution may not transfer to your new institution. Understanding how transferring will affect your current standing regarding your scholarships and loans is essential.

Furthermore, it is vital to research the new school's admissions requirements and familiarize yourself with your course catalog to determine if any credits earned from your prior institution are transferrable. Additionally, it is necessary to consider whether there are prerequisites for required courses before taking certain classes in the new school. Missing requirements may cause you to be behind in your studies when transferring.

It is also essential to assess if the new school's campus life and culture better fit you than your current institution. Attending classes on a new campus can be difficult if the environment does not match your expectations. Before deciding to transfer, you should discuss your situation with your school's academic and financial advisors. By assessing all these potential factors, you can make an informed decision about whether transferring is the best choice for you.

Conclusion

Pre-semester activities are essential to new students who want to determine the available resources at the institution and whether the school is a good fit for them. Talking to campus community members such as current students and alums, faculty, and staff can help you better understand the campus environment and culture. Some students may decide to live on campus while attending class; however, other students may commute. Commuter students have resources and opportunities to keep them connected to the school and its activities.

Although many students are happy at their institutions, some may find thriving at an institution difficult and may want to transfer. If you desire to transfer, research the implications of changing schools to your financial aid and program completion. All in all, you should thoroughly investigate any school you are thinking about enrolling in. You should visit the campus to learn about the resources and opportunities available to determine if the school has the resources to set you up for success.

Activate Your A.C.E.S.

Write short phrases on the lines provided. Use the Definition Box to help you.

1. **A**chievement-driven. What is your life goal?
   a. Explain how you want your life set up on your first day of classes.

   _____

   _____

   _____

   _____

   _____

   _____

   _____

   _____

   _____

   _____

New Student Orientation— An opportunity for new and prospective students to learn more about the institution. https://www.bestcolleges.com/blog/college-orientation-need-to-know/

Institutional Fit—How well a college, university, or some other entity meets the needs of a prospective student and how well the prospective student can connect with the campus culture. https://www.forbes.com/sites/willarddix/2016/05/09/what-college-match-and-fit-are-all-about/?sh=8c653f56d1fa

   b. Describe the resources you want to have on your first day of classes.

   _____

   _____

   _____

   _____

   _____

   _____

_____
_____
_____
_____

2. Capacity-informed. What resources do you have
   or need to get?
   a. Explain why you are a good fit for the
      institution you selected.

   _____
   _____
   _____
   _____
   _____
   _____
   _____
   _____

   b. Explain why the institution you selected is
      a good fit for you.

   _____
   _____
   _____
   _____

_____
_____
_____
_____

3. <u>E</u>nthusiasm-oriented. What motivates you?
   a. Explain your motivation for attending college.

_____
_____
_____
_____
_____
_____
_____
_____

4. <u>S</u>kill-building-focused. What current skills do you have? What skills do you need to gain?
   a. Use the campus scavenger hunt to identify the essential campus locations and resources listed.
      1. Campus Do-It-Yourself Scavenger Hunt—Take time to provide responses to the questions below to help you become familiar with your institution.

1. What are the institution's core values?
2. What is the institution's Mission Statement?
3. What is the institution's Vision Statement?
4. Where is the institution's Financial Aid Office located?
5. Where is the institution's Office of the Bursar located?
6. Where is the institution's Counseling Center located?
7. Where is the institution's learning assistance center/writing center/tutoring center located, and what areas are tutors available?
8. Where is the abilities office for students needing reasonable disability accommodations located?
9. Where is your department located?
10. Where is your preferred parking lot?
11. What does college or university accreditation mean?

12. Which entity accredits the institution? Is the institution accredited regionally or nationally?
13. Is the program you are enrolling in accredited?
14. Where is the institution's bookstore?
15. Where is the institution's career development center located?
16. Where is the institution's library located?
17. Where is the institution's cafeteria located?
18. Where is the institution's maintenance office located?
19. Where are the institution's student housing office and dorm rooms located?
20. Where is the institution's parking office located?
21. Where is the institution's public safety or police department located?
22. Where is the institution's office of records and registration located?
23. Where is the Office of the Registrar located?

24. Where is the Department of Student Affairs located?
25. Where is the institution's Veterans Affairs Office located?
26. Where is the institution's Wellness/Health Center located?
27. What is the physical address of the institution?
28. How do students living on campus receive their mail?
29. Where do students living on campus go to vote for general and national elections?

_____

_____

_____

_____

_____

_____

_____

_____

_____

_____

b. List the resources you currently use to help you manage your pre-semester activities.

_____

_____

_____

_____

_____

_____

_____

_____

_____

c. List the resources you need to help you manage your pre-semester activities but do not have.

_____

_____

_____

_____

_____

_____

_____

_____

d. Create an action plan to get access to the resources you need to access these resources.

_____

_____

_____

_____

_____

_____

_____

_____

_____

_____

The A.C.E.S. Framework™ Check-In

Now that you know more about pre-semester activities and have deepened your understanding of this topic, take what you learned and find out how it applies to your life.

Be sure to explore the related topics and resources on https://tracycrumpenterprisesllc.com/media-press.

There, you will find a wealth of information on pre-semester activities, so take your time to brush up on what you have learned here and expand your knowledge.

In addition, be sure to stop by our social media pages and let us know what your three takeaways from this chapter were. Relating the material to your unique experience is one of the best ways to get started on your path to success.

TheACESFramework

@ACESFramework

www.linkedin.com/in/tracygcrump

Chapter 6
Negotiate Personal, Roommate, and Professional
Relationships
How to Set Boundaries without Ruining Bonds

> "Relationships are important in
> school and at work."
> ~ Jessica M., college junior

A recent *CampusWell* survey found more than 25 percent of respondents indicated balancing life's competing responsibilities and their schoolwork was challenging, but students could do it successfully with planning and implementation. As with many other aspects of life, making an excellent first impression is vital in college when attempting to establish a personal, roommate, or professional relationship. Making a good impression means, after initially meeting you, a person leaves with a good feeling, a reasonable opinion, and the sense that you demonstrated an appropriate response in verbal and non-verbal communication during the interaction.

To make an excellent first impression, you should be honest and authentic with each interaction. It would also be helpful to learn how to navigate the multicultural world. Institutions of higher education attract faculty, staff, and students from all over the world to learn, grow, and discover their relationships within the global society. Therefore, interacting with people from different cultures and backgrounds will require some level of exposure and understanding of individuals and cultures that may be dissimilar from your own. As a college student, you can adopt helpful practices to assist you in navigating personal friendships, shared living relationships, and professional connections.

Making New Friends

Making new friends can be a rewarding experience. Forming relationships that allow you and the other person to add value to each other's lives can result in long-term friendships that extend beyond the college experience. These relationships can assist in helping you grow your personal and professional networks. Engaging in new relationships will sometimes require stepping outside your comfort zone to experience something new.

Making friends in college can be delicate, but it does not need to be overly complicated. An excellent way to make new friends is by finding common interests and activities to enjoy. Joining a student organization or club can help connect individuals with similar interests. Additionally, taking the time to try new things outside your comfort zone can connect you with others who share common hobbies and interests. It is also crucial that you remain authentic when meeting new people. You should not pretend to be someone else just to fit in. Your unique characteristics and attributes are what make you enjoyable. Be sure to let potential friends see your authentic self and experience all the fantastic benefits of having you in their circle.

Navigating a Shared Living Environment with Roommates

Having roommates can present an excellent opportunity to learn and grow; however, a few nuances are required to maintain a positive shared living environment. In some cases, you may have one roommate. In other cases, you may have more than one. Students who have strong positive familial support and positive friendship support experience less loneliness while attending college. Roommates present an excellent opportunity to establish longstanding bonds with friends while attending college; however, there are some essential boundaries and clarifications that must be understood when entering a shared living arrangement. Do not touch things that do not belong to you without permission. If either roommate allows the other to borrow something, saying "yes" one time is only "yes" for that time, not forever. Maintain proper hygiene (have the conversation, because different cultures do different things). Discuss whether outside shoes will be worn in the room.

Regarding guests coming or staying over, you and your roommates must establish ground rules at the outset of the roommate relationship. Discuss the personal items you will be okay with having in the open if people come over. Alternatively, discuss the personal things that should never be left in the open.

You and your roommates will also need to discuss whether you prefer the unit/room to be electronically monitored (i.e., security cameras). Similarly, if either roommate is involved in an intimate relationship, the parameters of the use of the shared space must be discussed. You also want to discuss social behaviors like having parties, smoking, drinking alcohol, television and music use, how early or late the lights will remain on or off, quiet hours, bedtime, wake-up time, and class schedules to allow you each sufficient time to prepare to leave.

If you or your roommates decide to consume alcohol, and you are of legal age to do so, be sure to responsibly consume alcohol (e.g., limiting yourself to not drinking to the point of getting drunk and not allowing alcohol to control your life and your relationships). Additionally, establish expectations around when to seek professional help if you or your roommates have potentially dangerous health or mental health issues.

Further, you and your roommates must discuss etiquette around the days and times you will come and go. Let your roommates know if you will not be in for the evening. Let your roommates know if you need the space privately so they can find alternative arrangements. Establish a cleaning schedule and concrete explanation of who will clean which areas and how often. Also, consider who will address cleaning issues beyond normal cleaning activities. Determine a cooking, dishwashing, and grocery shopping routines. Each roommate should know whether dishes are shared or owned and washed independently, whether grocery shopping and groceries are shared, or if each roommate is responsible for their own groceries and not expected to eat the other roommates' food. Likewise, determine a garbage disposal schedule.

Sharing a living space also requires proactive, creative measures regarding space and communication. At the outset, you and your roommates should designate exclusive and shared spaces for storage and clothes in closets, cabinets, and other areas in the unit. Establish each roommate's preferred method of communication if something comes up and a roommate needs the room for privacy. Additionally, you and your roommates should establish the preferred method of communication for emergencies, and exchange points of contact and information. Also, establish expected behavior for a roommate who becomes ill (e.g., do you stay in the unit and isolate, do you go home, can you use assistive aides like a humidifier, etc.?).

While each roommate hopes to have a challenge-free roommate experience, issues are likely to arise. Understanding how to navigate differences can support each roommate in having your interests heard, hearing your roommates' concerns, and working toward an amicable solution that can assist in preserving the relationship. If there is a problem, address it immediately and do not let it fester. Addressing issues as soon as they arise allows each party to understand concerns. It also decreases the likelihood that the problem will grow without the other roommate knowing there is an issue.

Navigating Professional Relationships

As with personal relationships, professional relationships are built on mutual respect, trust, and communication. You may need to build formal, professional relationships with faculty, staff, mentors, peers, possible employers, and others you may conduct business with in the future. Peers and colleagues must feel their unique talents are understood and appreciated, and that each person's opinions are considered when making decisions, they must feel they are in an environment that allows them to be open and honest, and they must believe their environment supports open dialogue to support accomplishing shared goals.

Several techniques could be adopted to keep building positive professional relationships, such as: understanding your needs and expectations from the professional relationship; creating a foundation of active participation that includes listening to each stakeholder's interests, concerns, and recommendations, and having appropriate space and opportunity to share your own interests, concerns, and suggestions; ensuring appropriate boundaries are articulated at the outset of the professional relationship; creating an environment that acknowledges success and shares gratitude; and avoiding negative, unproductive behaviors and communication that do not support reaching the shared goal.

Many people establish professional relationships to create a "value add" because they believe they can add and receive a benefit by being in the relationship. Value can be gained externally (e.g., monetary value, such as earning pay) or internally (e.g., an intrinsic value, such as acquiring a growth opportunity). Therefore, forming professional relationships is beneficial to each person and developing and nurturing it is important to everyone.

To maintain a productive professional relationship, you should identify areas where you can add value due to your unique skill set and offer to use your skills, ensure you are devoting time to actively sharing and learning from your colleagues, demonstrate your skills (do not just talk about them) as you are providing value to your peers, and keep the lines of communication open to create an environment that supports open dialogue and problem-solving.

Conclusion

Making a good impression is essential when establishing personal, roommate, and professional relationships. Being honest about who you are, your likes and dislikes, and the value you add to the relationship are critical to establishing and maintaining the connection. Having intercultural competence can assist in navigating relationships with people from cultures that may be dissimilar from your own. Many relationships you form in college last well beyond your college years and could result in decades-long friendships or professional endeavors. Therefore, it is essential to establish trusting, positive, healthy relationships from the start.

> **Personal Relationship**—Close, informal connections people form with each other based on private interactions and emotional ties. https://www.tonyrobbins.com /love-relationships/guide-to-personal-relationships/
> **Professional Relationship**— Formal connections created between people working together for a common purpose. https://www.indeed.com/care er-advice/career-development/professional-relationship

Activate Your A.C.E.S.

Write short phrases on the lines provided. Use the Definition Box to help you.

1. **A**chievement-driven. What is your life goal?
    a. Describe List the behaviors you expect from your personal friends and family members.

_____

_____

_____
_____
_____
_____
_____
_____

b. List the behaviors you will not tolerate
    from your personal friends and family
    members.

_____
_____
_____
_____
_____
_____
_____

c. List the behaviors you expect from people
    you live with.

_____
_____

_____
_____
_____
_____
_____
_____
_____

d. List the behaviors you will not tolerate
   from people you live with.

_____

_____

_____

_____

_____

_____

e. List the behaviors you expect from your
   professional colleagues.

_____

_____

_____

_____
_____
_____
_____
_____
_____
_____

    f. List the behaviors you will not tolerate from your professional colleagues.

_____
_____
_____
_____
_____
_____
_____

2. Capacity-informed. What resources do you have or need to get?
    a. List Explain how you interact with your family members and your relationship with them.

_____
_____

_____
_____
_____
_____
_____
_____

b. Explain how you interact with your friends
    and your relationship with them.

_____
_____
_____
_____
_____
_____

c. Explain how you interact with the people
    you live with and your relationship with
    them.

_____
_____

_____

_____

_____

_____

_____

_____

d. Explain how you interact with your professional colleagues and your relationship with them.

_____

_____

_____

_____

_____

_____

_____

_____

3. **E**nthusiasm-oriented. What motivates you?
   a. List Explain what motivates you to have positive relationships with your family members.

_____

_____

_____

_____

_____

_____

_____

_____

_____

_____

b. Explain what motivates you to have positive relationships with your friends.

_____

_____

_____

_____

_____

_____

_____

_____

c. Explain what motivates you to have positive relationships with the people you live with.

_____

_____

_____

_____

_____

_____

_____

_____

_____

_____

d. Explain what motivates you to have positive relationships with your professional colleagues.

_____

_____

_____

_____

_____

_____

_____

_____

_____

4. <u>S</u>kill-building-focused. What current skills do you have? What skills do you need to gain?
   a. List the resources you currently have to help you negotiate your personal, roommate, and professional relationships.

   _____
   _____
   _____
   _____
   _____
   _____
   _____
   _____
   _____
   _____

   b. List the resources you need to help you negotiate your personal, roommate, and professional relationships but do not have.

   _____
   _____
   _____
   _____
   _____
   _____
   _____

_____
_____

   c. Create an action plan to get access to the resources you need to access these resources.

_____
_____
_____
_____
_____
_____
_____
_____

The A.C.E.S. Framework™ Check-In

Now that you know more about navigating personal, roommate, and professional relationships and have deepened your understanding of this topic, take what you learned and find out how it applies to your life.

Be sure to explore the related topics and resources on https://tracycrumpenterprisesllc.com/media-press.

There, you will find a wealth of information on navigating personal roommate, and professional relationships, so take your time to brush up on what you have learned here and expand your knowledge.

In addition, be sure to stop by our social media pages and let us know what your three takeaways from this chapter were. Relating the material to your unique experience is one of the best ways to get started on your path to success.

TheACESFramework

@ACESFramework

www.linkedin.com/in/tracygcrump

Chapter 7
Productivity
Let's Get it Done

> "Professors want assignments that are well done and submitted on time. Having a plan for being productive is key to passing classes."
> ~ Stacey L.,
> college senior

Iris Reading contributor Lorea Lastiri states there is agreement in research that students who strategically plan to concentrate on completing assignments and course projects and on studying for assessments are more productive and have better learning outcomes than students who approach their coursework without deliberate preparation. The importance of productivity—consistently engaging in behaviors to allow you to achieve a specific result or outcome—in college cannot be understated. You can be productive if you actively evaluate and improve your resources and skills to achieve your goals.

Advancements in technology have allowed people to be more productive. As a college student, you use a variety of technological advancements when engaging with your peers and professors to increase your productivity. When using technology, there are expectations governing appropriate communication that all students must be aware of. You can set yourself up for success by planning how you will attend and interact in your courses and by familiarizing yourself with your course materials, course syllabi, course grade book, and institutional transcripts.

The Technology Used in College

In college, one tool used to increase productivity is institutional technology. Therefore, you should become familiar with each of the technological tools your institution makes available to increase student success, such as:

- your learning management system (LMS) (e.g., Blackboard, Canvas, Moodle, etc.),
- slide deck/presentation software,
- word-processing and spreadsheet applications,
- assessment tools (e.g., Respondus, Exam Soft),
- grading software, and
- assignment and originality software (e.g., Turn It In, SafeAssign, etc.).

Schools also have online library databases that allow you to access:

- books and journal articles (e.g., EBSCOhost),
- video conferencing software to aid virtual communication (e.g., Zoom, Microsoft Teams,
- GoToMeeting, Google Meet, Cisco Webex, etc.),
- cloud-based storage options (e.g., Dropbox),
- online research tools (e.g., SPSS, Qualtrics, ATLAS.ti, etc.), and
- a host of other tools.

It is a good practice for you to familiarize yourself with the technological resources available on campus within the first days of arriving.

General Communication

To be productive you must learn to communicate in various settings. Communication on a college campus takes place in person and online. The impressions communication leave on all parties shapes the present interaction and set the foundation for the future of relationships. As such, you also must navigate face-to-face etiquette and online netiquette. Remember: If you put it online, it will remain forever. There are several areas to be mindful of when communicating in class, on campus, via telephone, via e-mail, on discussion boards, and chat applications, and while interacting in online courses—whether synchronous (learning environments where you and the instructor engage in learning at the same time) or asynchronous (learning environments where you and the instructor engage in learning at different times).

You are expected to be respectful in all communications, even when discussing topics about which parties may disagree. You are expected to use appropriate language, style, and tone; refrain from using personal attacks; and provide academic support when making assertions. You are expected to evaluate your sources' credibility to ensure that your information has been assessed in an educational forum (generally through peer review). You are expected to refrain from profanity, impolite behavior, aggressive contact, or yelling. (For example, typing in all caps is considered shouting when presented in texts, chats, discussion forums, or other text-based communications.)

It would help if you used appropriate spelling, syntax, and grammar in all communications. You are expected to proofread all communications before sending or submitting the communication or assignment. Finally, you are expected to show yourself and others grace and forgiveness. Throughout interactions in college, non-verbal and verbal communication may present opportunities for misunderstanding. If something offends you, work with the person who communicated to address the offense. Likewise, if you offend someone, acknowledge your shortcomings (where applicable) and work with the person offended to address the issue.

Planning Your Class Schedule
Schedule planning is essential to ensure you remain on track to graduate in the time frame you desire and will be an invaluable skill when in the workforce. Generally, you need to complete a certain number of credits per semester, trimester, or quarter to ensure you graduate in four years. For example, a student on the semester schedule must complete 15 credit hours each semester, or 12 credit hours each fall and spring semester and six credit hours in the summer, May-term (Spring II), or J-Term (Winter) semester to remain on track toward graduation in four years. Because the credit hour requirement differs from school to school, each student must ensure they are successfully enrolling in and passing the required number of courses to keep them on track toward graduation. Be sure to work with your general advisor or academic

advisor (discipline advisor) to determine the appropriate number of credits you need to complete each semester to meet your graduation goal.

One technique that has demonstrated promise is ensuring you are enrolled in classes when you are optimally able to learn (i.e., the best time you identify for you to learn). For example, if you are a "morning lark" at your peak learning environment in the morning, schedule your classes back-to-back earlier in the day or afternoon. This schedule also works well if you need or want to work or have other responsibilities later in the day or evening. Contrastingly, if you are a "hummingbird," a person at their peak learning environment in the afternoon or the evening, schedule your classes back-to-back later in the day. Conversely, if you are a "night owl," you may enjoy a schedule with night classes. Further, if you are a person who needs to take a break after each class, schedule your classes to allow a pause between each course.

It is essential to find out when class schedules will be published so you can select the classes you want. Class enrollment is granted on a first-come basis, and when classes fill, students who did not enroll and want to complete the course will need to wait until the class is offered again. This means that students who register early in the registration cycle will likely get to enroll in the classes they want. In contrast, students who enroll later may be left with less-than-desirable class choices. Sometimes, the course you wish (or need) to enroll in may be offered at a different time than your preferred time or during your peak performance time. In these cases, you may need to plan to use additional resources or modify your social, personal, or work schedule to attend class, complete your coursework, and engage in all the required course tasks to allow you to be successful.

Please familiarize yourself with the required courses to complete your degree and when they are offered. Meet with your advisor before scheduling your courses. Create an alternative list of courses in case your first-choice course is unavailable. Determine the best time to retain information and plan your classes accordingly. Do not postpone general education course requirements (it is best to complete required courses early in your educational journey—preferably in your first and second years).

The Course Syllabus
One surefire way to be productive in college is to understand the course syllabus for each of your classes. The course syllabus is an essential document that describes the course policies, procedures, and requirements. Generally, the syllabus is a contract that binds the instructor and students enrolled in the course to its terms and conditions. Read the syllabus for each class several times. Ask questions about the syllabus to ensure you understand each of the requirements. Topics discussed in the syllabus include:

- Course name, number, section, semester, meeting times, days, meeting location, and format.
- Instructor name, title, rank, office location, office phone number, and e-mail address.

- Instructor preferred contact method and expected response time.
- Instructor office hours.
- Names and contact information for teaching/research assistants.
- Course catalog description.
- Course goals and learning objectives.
- Required textbooks and resources
- Recommended textbooks and resources.
- Resources held on reserve in the institutional library or at other locations.
- Pre- and co-requisites for the course.
- Course topics to be discussed.
- Assigned readings.
- Assignment, quiz, and examination due dates.
- Non-attendance dates.
- Methods used to evaluate student course task submissions.
- Enrolled students' expected interaction, behaviors, and course task submission policies.
- Explanation of how the final grade points, percentages, and letter grades will be computed.
- Late assignment policy.
- Revision assignment policy (if allowed).
- Procedure for requesting an incomplete final grade.
- Attendance policy.
- Academic integrity policy.
- Accommodations policy for students with special needs.

- Institutional support services (e.g., tutoring, learning, or writing center; health center, counseling center, etc.).
- Note-taking and study tips.
- Other helpful ancillary resources.

Setting the Foundation for a Substantial Course Performance

Rent or buy your textbooks <u>before</u> classes begin. If you buy your texts and will not need them in the future, consider selling them to earn extra money. Begin reading the introductory chapters of your textbooks *before* the first day of class. Ask your professor, the teaching assistant, or the institution's tutoring/learning center staff when you have questions or do not understand a topic.

One of the best predictors of course success is attendance and participation in course activities. As such, it is important to leave for and arrive at class early (you need time to get settled and prepare yourself to learn). While in class, remove all non-class distractions. Attendance is required. Select a seat that will assist you in accessing the course materials, participating in class, and being your most productive. Write a short introduction that tells your professors and classmates who you are. Many professors will ask for this. Here's a possible introduction formula:

- Name
- City and state
- Major
- Career aspirations

- Favorite movie
- Favorite book
- A place you would like to visit

Be sure to complete your day's reading *before* the class when the professor will cover the lesson. Doing so will allow you to ask questions if you have them. Try to answer questions when the professor asks them. However, you do not always need to be the first to respond or be the student who answers every question. You must find creative ways to learn, participate, and interact in your courses.

Submit all course assignments and tasks on time, using the required submission method, and containing the necessary information. You would also benefit from checking, double-checking, and triple-checking that your assignment submissions were correctly submitted and represented your best and final work.

Reading Grades
Understanding your college grade report is an integral part of successful academic performance and evaluating your productivity. As a college student, you will have a continuous "grade book" in each class and a transcript grade report for all courses you attempt while enrolled. Your class grade report provides a snapshot of your progress in the class, and your transcript offers a snapshot of your academic progress over your college career, including grades in courses taken and any credit hours earned. Your transcript also includes information about the terms and semesters you have attended and other details such as cumulative grade point average (GPA),

major or minor departments, transfer credits, and warnings/probations.

Understanding your GPA is essential in helping you determine your academic standing and the potential opportunities for furthering your education. You can calculate your GPA by dividing the total number of quality points earned in a semester or year of study by the total number of credit hours attempted. It measures overall performance during a given period. It serves as an indicator of how successful you have been in your studies. Many schools and jobs believe that a higher GPA represents dedication, motivation, and hard work, making it beneficial for students applying for graduate programs, internships, scholarships, and jobs.

A higher GPA reflects positively on your work ethic, dedication, and ability to succeed academically. Depending on the desired program or position, having a good GPA may be necessary or beneficial to gaining acceptance. In addition, students with higher GPAs tend to receive more awards, including academic honors and scholarships. Your GPA is also an excellent way to evaluate your progress over time to make any necessary changes or improvements if needed. By understanding the importance of your GPA and how it can affect future educational opportunities, you can better equip yourself to reach your goals.

Understanding Your Transcript
A college transcript is an official record of your academic history and helps you evaluate your productivity. It

contains information about courses taken, grades received, and any other honors or awards received while enrolled. Your college transcript should include basic information such as your name, school name, enrollment date, graduation date (if applicable), degree(s) earned, major(s) and minor(s), and courses taken. It should also include your cumulative grade point average GPA (your overall earned GPA averaged across all courses attempted).

When reviewing your transcript, it is essential to consider all components to gain an understanding of your overall academic standing. Examining each course line item can help you identify areas of weakness and progress. Paying attention to your cumulative GPA is vital in determining eligibility for scholarships, internships, awards, and overall progress toward graduation. It is also essential to consider any academic or probationary warnings issued by the university, which may indicate that you need to make changes to meet expectations.

Further, having a clear understanding of your grade report can help you make informed decisions about course selection and strategies when planning future semesters. Additionally, staying up to date on your grades can provide insight into how well you are doing relative to your goals and expectations. Suppose there is a discrepancy between what appears on your grade report and what appears on your transcripts. In that case, you must be proactive and contact the record's office to ensure that all information is accurate. It is an excellent practice to review your transcript regularly so that you can be aware of your standing and address any issues promptly. Paying attention to and understanding the contents of your college grades is an integral part of successful academic performance and helps ensure that your transcript reflects your effort.

Conclusion
Being productive in college is vital to ensure you progress as intended and work towards your graduation goals. Knowing the technological resources available on campus and how to access and use them create a strong foundation for success. Additionally, plan your strategy for attending and interacting in class and understand how to read and evaluate your transcripts. Being proactive can support your class performance and help you know your standing at the institution.

Activate Your A.C.E.S.

Write short phrases on the lines provided. Use the Definition Box to help you.

> **Productivity**—Progress a person makes toward meeting a goal.
> https://productivityreport.org/what-is-productivity/

1. Achievement-driven. What is your life goal?
   a. Describe your ideal seating choice when attending class.

_____

_____

_____
_____
_____
_____
_____
_____
_____

b. Explain what productivity looks like for you.

_____
_____
_____
_____
_____
_____
_____

2. <u>C</u>apacity-informed. What resources do you have or need to get?

   a. Explain whether you are a "morning lark" (you do your best work in the morning), a "hummingbird" (you do your best work in the afternoon), or a "night owl" (you do your best work at night).

_____
_____
_____
_____
_____
_____
_____
_____
_____
_____

3. **E**nthusiasm-oriented. What motivates you?
   a. Explain what motivates you to be productive.

_____
_____
_____
_____
_____
_____
_____
_____
_____
_____

4. **S**kill-building-focused. What current skills do you have? What skills do you need to gain?
    a. Make a schedule with five classes (1-hour each) that span your ideal week.

    _____
    _____
    _____
    _____
    _____
    _____
    _____
    _____

    b. Write the days and times you will not register for classes because it would be hard for you to do your best.

    _____
    _____
    _____
    _____
    _____
    _____
    _____
    _____
    _____

c. Write a template introduction that lists your name, city and state, major, career aspirations, favorite movie, favorite book, and a place you would like to visit.

_____
_____
_____
_____
_____
_____
_____
_____
_____

d. List the productivity resources you currently have.

_____
_____
_____
_____
_____
_____
_____
_____

e. List the productivity resources you need
    but do not have.

    _____
    _____
    _____
    _____
    _____
    _____
    _____
    _____

f. Create an action plan to access the
    resources you need to increase your
    productivity.

    _____
    _____
    _____
    _____
    _____
    _____
    _____
    _____

The A.C.E.S. Framework™ Check-In

Now that you know more about productivity and have deepened your understanding of this topic, take what you learned and find out how it applies to your life.

Be sure to explore the related topics and resources on https://tracycrumpenterprisesllc.com/media-press.

There, you will find a wealth of information on productivity, so take your time to brush up on what you have learned here and expand your knowledge.

In addition, be sure to stop by our social media pages and let us know what your three takeaways from this chapter were. Relating the material to your unique experience is one of the best ways to get started on your path to success.

TheACESFramework

@ACESFramework

www.linkedin.com/in/tracygcrump

Chapter 8
Time Management/Prioritizing Your Competing Responsibilities:
Making the Most of Every 24 Hours to Get Things Done without Running out of Time

> "There is so much to do in college. You must stay on top of everything if you want success."
> ~ Peter B., college senior

A ccording to Deyan Georgiev, a *Techjury* contributor, almost 90 percent of college students could have higher grades if they implemented better time and task management routines. Managing time in college is one of the highest reward activities you can undertake. Prioritizing tasks and time will allow you to understand your commitments better, ensure you are where you are supposed to be when you are supposed to be, and guarantee you do not miss important deadlines. As a college student, you can use traditional calendars or electronic task-managing systems to keep yourself organized and prioritize your competing responsibilities.

Prioritizing Your Time

Time management is a skill that requires constant development and consideration of your competing responsibilities. Managing time will allow you to prioritize tasks, use available resources better, and reduce stress. Taking a few minutes each week to plan out your activities for the upcoming days and weeks will help you achieve balance by allowing you to see what needs to be done and to determine which tasks take priority over others.

To manage your time, you need to manage your physical and emotional state and master the ability to focus on tasks and responsibilities in isolation. Use a calendar to schedule everything in your life (see Figure 9). Items you may consider adding to your calendar are:

- Personal time,
- Social time,
- Downtime,
- Time to complete homework,
- Class attendance time,
- Work time,
- Time to eat, and
- Time to sleep.

Figure 9: Sample Schedule

	Sunday	Monday	Tuesday	Wednesday	Thursday	Friday	Saturday
7:00 AM	Breakfast	Breakfast	Breakfast	Breakfast	Breakfast	Breakfast	Breakfast
8:00 AM							
9:00 AM							
10:00 AM		ART-100	HISTORY-100	ART-100	HISTORY-100	ART-100	
11:00 AM		Study	Study	Study	Study	Study	
12:00 PM							
1:00 PM		BIOLOGY-100		BIOLOGY-100		BIOLOGY-100	
2:00 PM			MATH-100		MATH-100		
3:00 PM	Work	ENGLISH-100					Work
4:00 PM		Study	Study	Study	Study	Study	
5:00 PM	Exercise		Exercise		Exercise		
6:00 PM	Dinner	Dinner	Dinner	Dinner	Dinner	Dinner	Dinner
7:00 PM		Study	Study	Study	Study	Study	
8:00 PM							
9:00 PM	Sleep	Sleep	Sleep	Sleep	Sleep	Sleep	Sleep
10:00 PM							

These are not the only categories to consider. However, each of the categories listed is important to your well-being. For example, ensuring you are adequately rested is the first step to be your most productive. Likewise, ensuring you eat a healthy diet that includes the recommended daily amounts of vegetables, healthy oils, whole grains, healthy proteins, fruits, and water is vital to promoting overall health. Healthy food choices are more manageable when you have options and pre-plan your meals using your scheduling system. Similarly, having scheduled time for physical activity and flex time on your calendar allow opportunities for you to maintain your physical health and take breaks or address an unplanned situation.

When creating your master calendar, schedule designated times to study during periods where you best retain information. Schedule time for breaks and time for yourself. Guard your time: You are only available if something is on your schedule. Consider using an electronic or a physical calendar, depending on your preferences. You can block time for class, work, and family time and get reminders about upcoming events and activities. You can add your schedule to your mobile device using an electronic calendar. Hence, you always know what is on your daily itinerary. Start each day strong by creating a routine that works best for you and your class schedule.

Setting realistic goals for yourself will help you establish achievable deadlines for completing assignments or studying for exams so you can manage your workload. Setting aside time for relaxation allows you to take regular breaks and supports relieving stress and maintaining focus. You can also use schedule time with a study group or time for tutoring sessions when needed to help you understand complicated material faster and increase your motivation to stay on task. Everyone is different, and it might take some trial and error to find the best approach for managing your time. Still, with practice, you can learn how to use your time wisely and succeed in your studies and life.

Conclusion
Adopting a time-management strategy that allows you to prioritize your tasks and responsibilities supports being proactive in successfully reaching your educational and career goals. Using a schedule can illustrate your obligations and commitments and can allow you to recognize times when you can relax and unwind. Advancements in technology will enable you to either record your schedule manually or electronically, to set

reminders if needed, to keep you on track, and to maintain a healthy and productive lifestyle.

Activate Your A.C.E.S.

Write short phrases on the lines provided. Use the Definition Box to help you.

> **Time Management**—How effectively a person uses their time to achieve a goal.
> https://dictionary.cambridge.org/us/dictionary/english/time-management

1. Achievement-driven. What is your life goal?
   a. Explain your goal for managing your time and competing responsibilities.

   _____
   _____
   _____
   _____
   _____
   _____
   _____
   _____
   _____
   _____

2. Capacity-informed. What resources do you have or need to get?

a. Describe how you currently manage your time and prioritize your competing responsibilities.

_____
_____
_____
_____
_____
_____
_____
_____
_____

3. Enthusiasm-oriented. What motivates you?
   a. Explain the benefits for your life if you manage your time and competing responsibilities.

_____
_____
_____
_____
_____
_____
_____
_____

_____

_____

4. **S**kill-building-focused. What current skills do you have? What skills do you need to gain?

    a. Create a 1-month calendar that has your personal time, social time, the time when you prefer to complete homework, the time when you are scheduled to attend class, the time where you are scheduled to work (if applicable), time to eat, the time when you plan to sleep, and any other time you need to schedule (e.g., alone time or break time, etc.).

       What kind of "write on lines" or visual prompt to act can I add here?

    b. List the time management resources you currently use.

_____

_____

_____

_____

_____

_____

_____

_____

_____

c. List the time management resources you need to maintain your time management but do not have.

_____
_____
_____
_____
_____
_____
_____
_____

d. Create an action plan to access the resources you need to optimize your time management.

_____
_____
_____
_____
_____
_____
_____
_____

The A.C.E.S. Framework™ Check-In

Now that you know more about time management and prioritizing your competing responsibilities and have deepened your understanding of this topic, take what you learned and find out how it applies to your life.

Be sure to explore the related topics and resources on https://tracycrumpenterprisesllc.com/media-press.

There, you will find a wealth of information on time management and prioritizing your competing responsibilities, so take your time to brush up on what you have learned here and expand your knowledge.

In addition, be sure to stop by our social media pages and let us know what your three takeaways from this chapter were. Relating the material to your unique experience is one of the best ways to get started on your path to success.

TheACESFramework

@ACESFramework
www.linkedin.com/in/tracygcrump

Part 3: Strategies for Future Success
Plan for Your WIN

Chapter 9
Harness Your Professors' Expertise
You've Got an Ace in the Hole, So Use It

"Professors can help you in
the class and outside of
class."
~ Kerry C.,
college sophomore

Sarah D. Sparks, an *EducationWeek* contributor, states that students who have professional connections with their professors have better education outcomes, including higher grades, more engagement, and increased attendance. It is well-known that college professors can help you in the classroom as you are learning the course material. However, faculty members may also assist you in gaining clarity during career exploration, offer educational or career options feedback, provide additional educational or research opportunities, create forums where you can share experiences and ask questions, and provide other mentorship opportunities.

Make Sure Your Professor Knows You and Your Career Goals
College students are fortunate to have access to the expertise and knowledge of professors. This valuable resource can be used outside the classroom in various ways. At all times, your relationship with your professors should remain professional and be focused on your goal

to obtain necessary information to help you succeed in college and in your career. One way is to take advantage of office hours. During office hours, you can consult with your professor regarding course materials or research topics related to the class.

Additionally, professors are often willing to provide advice and guidance on student-led projects or internships. Professors can also be a great source of career advice and networking opportunities. By utilizing your professor's expertise outside the classroom, you can gain valuable insight into your field of study and develop essential skills for post-graduation life. However, before taking advantage of your professor's expertise outside the classroom, you must first ensure your professor knows you and your career goals.

Introduce yourself to your professor so the professor knows who you are. Tell your professor your first and last name, your major, and why you are enrolled in the course. Ensuring your professor knows who you are can assist when opportunities arise (e.g., scholarships, grants, networking, jobs, etc.) that fit your skillset or when you need letters of recommendation. Be sure to use the course syllabus to learn where your professor's office is and how you should best contact your professor. Some prefer e-mails, and others prefer telephone calls. Ask your professor which contact method they like if it is not listed on the course syllabus. Be sure to ask questions outside of class.

When interacting with your professor outside of class, be sure to have a specific topic to discuss. For example, if you have an "educational future" question, be sure you have researched your options to allow you to answer questions about your needs and expectations if asked. Similarly, if you have a "career" question, be sure you know the general occupation industry, job title, and requirements to allow you to discuss the opportunity in detail.

College Professors Can Help You Gain Educational and Career Clarity

College professors can provide the educational and career clarity you need to succeed and offer mentorship. One of the most important things college professors can do is to provide you with an understanding of the types of jobs available in your field to gain insights into what your future could look like. College professors can create opportunities for you to have an open dialogue about job opportunities, internships, and educational programs that may be available. You must understand what types of resources are available in your field or even outside of it, which can help you gain greater insight into possible career paths. If your college professor knows your interests and aspirations, your professor can better assist you.

College professors can also provide mentorship so you can better understand how to apply for jobs or internships. This type of mentorship could involve helping you access university career services resources to create resumés and cover letters as well as directing you to institutional resources to help them prepare for interviews, so you feel more confident when talking with potential employers or representatives from graduate programs. Likewise, college professors could write recommendation letters on your behalf to support your applications. It would help if you only asked for recommendation letters from professors you have a positive relationship with and who can attest to your superior educational abilities.

Additionally, college professors could host alumni panel sessions to allow former students to discuss their post-graduate experiences to shed light on post-graduation education and employment opportunities. Furthermore, college professors could connect you with relevant resources and tools such as internship websites, job boards, and databases related to your field so you can search for opportunities more effectively and efficiently. Moreover, faculty members could also suggest professional organizations or associations related to your chosen profession, allowing you to gain knowledge about new industry trends or create networking opportunities with other professionals or mentors who can offer additional guidance.

Another helpful practice college professors employ is creating classes dedicated to helping you prepare for potential careers. Through discussion-based courses such as professional writing workshops or even simply engaging lectures on topics relevant to specific industries, faculty have an excellent opportunity to guide you toward a successful future by introducing you to course material and inspiring discussions about different perspectives related to the field.

A Note about Implementation
Professors can help you access critical information and resources that benefit your future success. However, you are solely responsible for using the resources and implementing strategies if you desire to be successful. As such, you should be prepared to use the resources and connections provided and take the initiative to develop concrete plans to prepare for the future.

Conclusion
Although college professors are known for providing educational support for the subjects they teach, they are also invaluable sources to help you explore your future academic aspirations and career endeavors. Professors can help you gain clarity and provide mentorship. Further, professors can help you access career service resources and write recommendation letters. To take advantage of your professors' expertise, know who you are and your goals and aspirations, communicate your goals to your professor, and be prepared to use the resources, suggestions, and connections given to help you achieve your goals.

Activate Your A.C.E.S.

Write short phrases on the lines provided. Use the Definition Box to help you.

1. <u>A</u>chievement-driven. What is your life goal?
   a. Explain your goals for interacting with your professors.

   _____
   _____

   _____
   _____
   _____
   _____
   _____
   _____
   _____

2. <u>C</u>apacity-informed. What resources do you have or need to get?
   a. Describe how you develop a positive, professional relationship with your professors/professors.

   _____
   _____
   _____

_____

_____

_____

_____

_____

_____

3. **E**nthusiasm-oriented. What motivates you?
   a. Explain what motivates you to have a positive, professional relationship with your professors.

   _____

   _____

   _____

   _____

   _____

   _____

   _____

   _____

4. **S**kill-building-focused. What current skills do you have? What skills do you need to gain?
   a. Write an "elevator pitch" to explain who you are, your goals, and how you would

like your professor to assist you in
reaching your goals.

_____

_____
_____
_____
_____
_____
_____
_____

b. List the resources you currently have to
help you connect with your professor.

_____

_____
_____
_____
_____
_____
_____
_____

c. List the resources you need to help you connect with your professor but do not have.

_____

_____

_____

_____

_____

_____

_____

_____

d. Create an action plan to access the resources you need to connect with your professor.

_____

_____

_____

_____

_____

_____

_____

_____

The A.C.E.S. Framework™ Check-In

Now that you know more about harnessing your professors' expertise and have deepened your understanding of this topic, take what you learned and find out how it applies to your life.

Be sure to explore the related topics and resources on https://tracycrumpenterprisesllc.com/media-press.

There, you will find a wealth of information on harnessing your professors' expertise, so take your time to brush up on what you have learned here and expand your knowledge.

In addition, be sure to stop by our social media pages and let us know what your three takeaways from this chapter were. Relating the material to your unique experience is one of the best ways to get started on your path to success.

TheACESFramework

@ACESFramework

www.linkedin.com/in/tracygcrump

Chapter 10
Access Support Resources:
Calling for Backup When You Need a Bigger Boat

> "Knowing about where to go when
> you have questions can help you
> avoid a lot of problems."
> ~ Zola M., college junior

EducationDynamics contributor Chris Gilmore notes using campus support resources can increase college retention rates by providing students with tools to help them overcome issues that may hinder their progress. Colleges and universities have many resources to assist you beyond those provided in the classroom.

You can access learning support resources, career preparation services, and occupational literacy information that you can use in school and the workforce. As a college student, you can utilize staff members' expertise in offering career advice, industry insights, research projects, financial literacy, or even general mentorship. These conversations could open networking opportunities, help further your understanding of your field, and create meaningful connections.

Campus Support Staff
Numerous staff members on college campuses can provide various types of support to increase your

opportunities for success. One of the first support personnel you should get to know is your course and institutional support staff. If your course has a teaching assistant, you should know their name and contact information. Generally, a teaching assistant can answer course-specific questions and provide insight about course activities, assessments, and grades. You should also get to know your academic advisor. Your academic advisor can help you understand your institutional records, evaluate your progress toward graduation, and recommend courses or activities you may benefit from.

If you are a student-athlete, you should get to know your support advisors. In addition to navigating college courses, student-athletes must also navigate their role as team members. The student-athlete support advisor can assist with making recommendations when you are preparing your course and athletics schedule, provide insight on methods student-athletes can use to persist in college and graduate according to their plans, provide advising support and information regarding any NCAA academic eligibility rules, and coordinate with the athletic staff, coaches, and student-athletes regarding opportunities for intellectual skill development and individualized support if needed.

It would help if you also got to know your information technology support team. Twenty-first-century colleges and universities use a wide array of technology. Students desiring to learn more about institutional technology resources, or those required to use the resources, should identify the location, e-mail address, telephone number, and hours of operation for the university's information technology office. Personnel in this office can assist when you need help setting up your college accounts or have issues accessing institutional resources.

International students can also access personalized support on a college campus. If you are an international student, you should identify where the international student center is as well as their e-mail address, telephone number, and hours of operation. You should also specify where English language (or ESL), tutoring, writing centers, and math labs are located.

Students desiring a faith-based experience should identify where on-campus spiritual support is located and obtain the office personnel's e-mail address, telephone number, and hours of operation. You should also remember all components of campus safety (campus police, safety, or security; blue light/emergency phones; campus alert systems; alert apps; escort/umbrella services, etc.) and ensure you know how to report incidents formally.

Be sure to locate your institution's learning center, disabilities' office, health center, and counseling center. Learning and writing center resources are available to any student who desires to improve in a subject or who wants to improve their writing. These services are not only available to students who are struggling. On that note, do not wait until you struggle to access learning or tutoring center services. You can get help learning about research, writing, editing, and revision techniques and have an assignment draft review and discussion of your strengths and opportunities for improvement. You can get help with most subjects. Ask the department chair or the dean if the center does not have a tutor assigned for the subject.

Additionally, if you need reasonable accommodations due to a disability, you should contact your campus disabilities office. These departments can collect information and evaluate your situation on a case-by-case basis. When registered with the disabilities' office, students receive reasonable accommodations to assist with being successful in their courses.

Likewise, be sure to know where the institutional health center is located and their hours of operation. The health center can provide services like those available at your primary care physician's office. Similarly, suppose you need emotional or psychological support or other mental health services. In that case, you can utilize the institution's counseling center to speak with professionals trained to address your needs. Be sure you know where their office is located and their hours of operation.

Conclusion
As a college student, you have access to many resources to help you in the classroom and beyond. Using learning support resources can help you learn and thrive in your courses and can help with understanding essential aspects of life. You can also utilize staff members' expertise to understand career options or gain mentorship. These resources and services can support you while enrolled in

college, and the information learned can be beneficial after graduation.

Activate Your A.C.E.S.

Write short phrases on the lines provided. Use the Definition Box to help you.

> **Campus Support Resources—** Supplemental services and materials designed to help students succeed.
> https://abound.college/finishcoll ege/advice/12-helpful-campus-resources-wes-creel/

10. <u>A</u>chievement-driven. What is your life goal?
  m. Describe your goals for accessing support resources.

_____

_____

_____

_____

_____

_____

_____

_____

_____

  n. Write the location of your campus safety/police department.

_____
_____
_____
_____
_____
_____
_____
_____
_____
_____

o. Write the location of your campus counseling center.

_____
_____
_____
_____
_____
_____
_____
_____

p. Write the location of your campus health center.

_____
_____

_____
_____
_____
_____
_____
_____
_____

q. Write the location of your campus learning, tutoring, or writing center.

_____
_____
_____
_____
_____
_____

r. Write the location of your campus career services office.

_____
_____

_____
_____
_____
_____
_____
_____
_____
_____

s. Write the location of any other campus
    support resource you will need.

_____
_____
_____
_____
_____
_____
_____

11. Capacity-informed. What resources do you have
    or need to get?
      m. Explain how you currently access
         resources for school.

_____
_____

_____
_____
_____
_____
_____
_____
_____
_____

12. **E**nthusiasm-oriented. What motivates you?
    m. Explain what motivates you to access resources for school.

_____
_____
_____
_____
_____
_____
_____
_____

13. **S**kill-building-focused. What current skills do you have? What skills do you need to gain?
    m. Write your plan for accessing support resources on campus.

_____

_____

_____

_____

_____

_____

_____

_____

_____

_____

The A.C.E.S. Framework™ Check-In

Now that you know more about accessing support resources and have deepened your understanding of this topic, take what you learned and find out how it applies to your life.

Be sure to explore the related topics and resources on https://tracycrumpenterprisesllc.com/media-press.

There, you will find a wealth of information on accessing support resources, so take your time to brush up on what you have learned here and expand your knowledge.

In addition, be sure to stop by our social media pages and let us know what your three takeaways from this chapter were. Relating the material to your unique experience is one of the best ways to get started on your path to success.

TheACESFramework

@ACESFramework

www.linkedin.com/in/tracygcrump

Chapter 11
Find Your Leadership Voice:
Wakey-Wakey, it's Time to Take the Lead

> "Making your mark on campus helps all
> the students but it also helps you get
> ready for the real world."
> ~ Diallo F., college senior

According to *Harvard Business Review* contributors Michael L. Anderson and Fangwen Lu, students benefit from early leadership experiences by learning skills that will help them in school and life. Anderson and Lu note that students in leadership positions experience better academic performance, increased confidence, and positive social relationships. Being a college student presents a unique opportunity to learn and grow. You are learning not only about the subjects you enroll in but also about yourself. You will be involved in campus activities that help you better understand your likes and dislikes and may find an area you are passionate about. Participating in teams, clubs, organizations, and other activities like shadow days, internships, and externships may benefit you, whether you live in the dorms or commute to campus.

Getting Involved on Campus
As a college student, you can take advantage of numerous opportunities to be involved in campus life and become a leader on campus. Developing leadership skills can help you gain valuable experience for your professional career

and provide opportunities to build meaningful connections with your peers. One excellent way to cultivate your leadership skills is to get involved in student organizations and clubs. These organizations provide the perfect platform for developing communication and management skills while also allowing you to network. Participating in student government can also be an effective way for you to sharpen your leadership abilities, as participation will enable you to work closely with other leaders. Additionally, attending relevant conferences or workshops focused on developing leadership skills can bolster your ability to be an effective leader.

As a college student, you can also take advantage of various leadership opportunities within your classes and departments. Serving as a teaching assistant is one such opportunity, which can help you develop strong communication and organizational skills by working directly with professors and other students in the class. Participating in research projects and taking independent study courses are additional ways to hone your leadership qualities while gaining valuable knowledge about your academic field.

You may also consider joining community service activities or clubs focusing on social change. These activities offer great potential for developing personal values, building relationships, and inspiring others through advocacy work. By engaging in these activities, you can become a leader within your communities while also building professional skills that will be beneficial in the future.

Teams, Clubs, and Organizations
You can gain numerous benefits from participating in teams, clubs, and organizations, such as developing social skills and meeting people with similar interests. Participating in these activities can also help build relationships with peers, promote self-confidence, and increase academic success.

One of the most significant benefits of joining teams, clubs, and organizations is that it helps develop social skills. Making new friends is one of the most critical parts of the college experience. Yet, many students need help to make close connections due to the unfamiliarity of the campus environment or a lack of confidence. Participating in activities such as sports teams, debate clubs, student government associations, or volunteer groups can provide an opportunity to meet like-minded individuals while also having fun. You can also learn to work with others and develop valuable interpersonal skills that will serve you well beyond college.

Participating in teams and other extracurricular activities also allows you to build meaningful relationships with your peers. This is especially important for first-year students who may have few friends. Being part of a club or team can give you a supportive base from which you can form strong friendships outside the classroom. These experiences can be beneficial because they allow you to work closely with teammates over long periods on projects or initiatives while engaging in meaningful conversations about shared interests or simply spending time together outside of classes.

Another benefit of participating in clubs and organizations during your higher education career is that it promotes self-confidence through positive reinforcement when achieving something worthwhile within a group setting. Gaining recognition among peers for contributing something beneficial, such as leading a discussion topic during a meeting or winning an award within a particular club, demonstrates that you are a valued member of society. This sense of accomplishment often translates into higher self-esteem, which will help you reach better success throughout your academic journey.

Participation in extracurricular activities may help academic performance due to the increased learning opportunities experienced mentors provide while developing teamwork skills. The structure provided by dedicated staff teaching good work ethics within environmental settings encourages discipline and responsibility among participants. These attributes often reflect positively on grades and other aspects of daily routines, such as attendance and study habits.

Take Advantage of Shadow Days, Internships, and Externships
Shadow days, internships, and externships are valuable opportunities to gain experience in your field. Participating in these activities can help you develop

skills that will benefit your future job searches. Shadowing an experienced professional allows you to observe how they work and learn the ins and outs of your profession. An internship or externship may provide hands-on training and mentorship from seasoned professionals. All these experiences can offer invaluable insight into what it takes to succeed in a particular industry. Additionally, participating in such activities can help build connections with industry leaders who can provide guidance or career opportunities.

Conclusion

Whether you live in the dormitory or commute to campus, numerous opportunities, on and off campus, allow you to get involved and help find your leadership voice. Participating in teams, clubs, organizations, shadow days, internships, and externships will not only enrich your college experience but also provide meaningful networking opportunities and help establish relationships and skill sets that could help propel your career success.

Activate Your A.C.E.S.

Write short phrases on the lines provided. Use the Definition Box to help you.

1. Achievement-driven.
   What is your life goal?
   a. Describe Explain what being a leader means to you.

Leadership—Being able to motivate, inspire, direct, supervise, and manage others toward meeting a common goal.
https://www.merriam-webster.com/dictionary/leadership

_____

_____

_____

_____

_____

_____

_____

_____

   b. Explain the type of leader you would like to be.

_____

_____

_____

_____

_____
_____
_____
_____
_____

c. Explain your goals for interacting with
    teams, clubs, and organizations.

_____
_____
_____
_____
_____
_____

d. Explain your goals for taking part in
    internships and externships.

_____
_____
_____
_____

_____
_____
_____
_____

2. Capacity-informed. What resources do you have
   or need to get?
   a. Describe the activities you currently do as
      a leader.

_____
_____
_____
_____
_____
_____
_____

   b. Describe the teams, clubs, and
      organizations you are currently in.

_____
_____
_____
_____

_____
_____
_____
_____

3. **E**nthusiasm-oriented. What motivates you?
   a. Explain what motivates you to be a leader.

   _____
   _____
   _____
   _____
   _____
   _____
   _____
   _____

   b. Explain what motivates you to be part of a
      team, club, or organization.

   _____
   _____
   _____
   _____
   _____

_____
_____
_____
_____

4. Skill-building-focused. What current skills do you
   have? What skills do you need to gain?
   a. List the teams, clubs, and organizations
      that interest you on campus.

   _____
   _____
   _____
   _____
   _____
   _____
   _____
   _____

   b. Make an appointment to speak to a
      representative of one of the teams, clubs,
      and organizations listed above to find out
      when they have an open meeting where
      you can learn more about them.

   _____
   _____

_____
_____
_____
_____
_____
_____
_____

c. List the professionals you would like to shadow to learn more about their jobs.

_____
_____
_____
_____
_____
_____

d. List the internships/externships you would like to apply for to learn more about your future career.

_____
_____

_____
_____
_____
_____
_____
_____
_____

e. List the leadership resources you currently
   have.

_____
_____
_____
_____
_____
_____
_____

f. List the leadership resources you need but
   do not have.

_____
_____
_____

_____
_____
_____
_____
_____
_____

g. Create an action plan to get access to the
   leadership resources you need.

_____
_____
_____
_____
_____
_____
_____

The A.C.E.S. Framework™ Check-In

Now that you know more about finding your leadership
voice and have deepened your understanding of this topic,
take what you learned and find out how it applies to your
life.

Be sure to explore the related topics and resources on https://tracycrumpenterprisesllc.com/media-press.

There, you will find a wealth of information on finding your leadership voice, so take your time to brush up on what you have learned here and expand your knowledge.

In addition, be sure to stop by our social media pages and let us know what your three takeaways from this chapter were. Relating the material to your unique experience is one of the best ways to get started on your path to success.

TheACESFramework

@ACESFramework

www.linkedin.com/in/tracygcrump

Chapter 12
Prepare for Career Success:
Are You Ready to Crush Your Competition

"The whole point of college is to get ready for your career. So, it's important to use the resources the college offers to help you get ready."
~ Mona G.,
college junior

Center on Budget and Policy Priorities contributors Chad Stone, Danilo Trisi, Arloc Sherman, and Jennifer Beltrán state college students who are unprepared for the workforce will experience inequitable educational opportunities and a more challenging time finding meaningful employment. As a college student, you have a host of new experiences and new information to navigate while attending school.

Some experiences help you learn and grow, and other experiences help you prepare for the workforce. Using the career services office, career fairs, mock interviews, alumni associations, and mentors could assist you in developing a personal statement, cover letter, and resumé and prepare you to network and interview. Accessing these resources will assist you in positioning your skills and expertise in the best light as you prepare for graduation and begin the job search process.

Career Services Office

As a college student, you should use the resources available at your institution's career services office to help prepare for your job search. Staff members can provide resources to assist you in gaining insight into various job opportunities. They can help you connect with potential employers. Career services staff can also assist you by providing resources to help you develop professional skills and create cover letters, resumés, personal statements, and portfolios that illustrate your expertise and abilities. Career services staff members also routinely help with securing internship opportunities, career readiness workshops, mock interview forums, networking events, and continuing education opportunities.

Career Fairs

Taking part in a career fair is an excellent opportunity for you to find out the positions that employers are hiring for and to network and build professional connections. Generally, career fairs allow you to go to a single location and meet with recruiters and business leaders from a wide array of industries. During the sessions, you can learn more about the company, its culture, its needs, and the specific skills ideal employees for open positions should have. When attending a career fair, you should come prepared by dressing business casual, being open to meaningful conversation, and being ready to participate in an interview and submit your resumé. Before the career fair, identify the businesses you will meet with and research them. You should note the companies' missions, visions, and goals, as well as their needs and expectations. This information should be available on the organizations' websites. Additionally, be sure to write down the names and contact information for each business representative you meet with so you can send them a thank you note or follow up message. Sending thank you notes and follow up messages add a personal touch to the interaction and could help to set you apart from other potential candidates.

Mock Interviews
Mock interviews allow you to practice process-oriented thinking, communication, and interview skills in a setting that mimics an actual job interview. When you participate in mock interviews, you should prepare as if you were meeting with a business representative from a company you want to work for. Research the company and record their mission, vision, and goals. It would help if you also explored newsworthy initiatives the company is involved in.

Further, you should identify the benefits you will bring to the company if hired. You should also dress business casual during the mock interview and be mindful of your verbal and non-verbal language throughout the interaction. The person conducting the interview is generally a staff or faculty member or an industry professional trained to assist in developing interview skills. During the mock interview, you will be asked questions just like in a job interview. After the mock interview, you can discuss your performance with the interviewer. You will be given feedback to help you develop as a job candidate. This level of interaction can assist you with gaining confidence in your ability to present yourself professionally.

Interviews

As you prepare for your job interview, research the company to understand its goals, values, and the qualities they want in potential candidates. Familiarizing yourself with the organization can help you demonstrate your interest in working with them.

You also want to review the job description and consider what skills and experiences you possess that make you the best fit for the role. Tailor your resume and cover letter to highlight those qualities. Potential employers are interested in candidates who can demonstrate how they can contribute meaningfully to the team.

You also want to spend time practicing for the interview. Practice common interview questions and be prepared to discuss your skills and experiences in detail. Additionally, prepare questions about the company or position before the interview to gain more insight into working environment and company culture.

Alumni Association

As a college student, you may also connect with your institution's alumni association to access meaningful resources from people who have graduated from the institution. Generally, alumni associations host networking and mentorship events that allow current students to connect with graduates, access career resources, learn about challenges and successes graduates experienced, and learn about strategies former students have used to navigate obstacles. Alumni association events may also provide opportunities to share information about open positions in various industries. After graduation, you can join the alumni association and mentor students in the future. This will allow you to stay connected to the institution and receive information about campus events, initiatives, and other news.

Mentors
Mentorship is vital to every college student. Mentors offer information and advice about how they navigated their education and career. You can find mentors within your current networks and in social and professional environments. For example, if there is someone you admire in your existing network—like a family member or friend, professor, or counselor—you may ask them to be your mentor.

You may also research professionals in your field and ask them to serve as your mentor. Likewise, professional organizations in your field may have mentorship programs. Other great places to find mentors are by attending professional association workshops, networking events, seminars, conferences, or community events. If you do not know which events to attend, consider reading professional trade magazine articles, newsletters, or blog posts written by thought leaders in your field. Further, you could look through your social media contacts to find out if any of your connections work in your field and could serve as your mentor.

Having a mentor will give you access to invaluable resources to help you complete your studies and understand the workforce. Generally, the mentorship relationship requires both the mentor and the mentee to be active participants. It would help if you always came to mentorship meetings prepared with questions you believe will benefit you in your studies or career. You and your mentors should set your agendas and boundaries early in the relationship to help establish expectations and goals. It would help if you were honest about your skills, needs, and challenges to allow the mentor to be as helpful as possible.

Personal Statement
As a college student, you should create a personal statement to allow you to reflect on what makes you unique, what your goals are, and what skills you possess that set you apart from others. The personal statement is generally a one- or two-page document (some organizations will ask for a specific word count) that explains your experiences, accomplishments, and suitability for a particular role. Personal statements allow you to explain how your life experiences shaped your personality and how you will use those experiences to add value to the organization.

Personal statements should refrain from regurgitating information contained in your other application materials. In contrast, your personal statement should add to the reader's understanding of your personality, characteristics, attributes, ideologies, philosophies, and values. Your personal statement should demonstrate why the organization will want to work with you. If the organization requires specific content to be included, be sure to include that content. Be sure to proofread your personal statement thoroughly to ensure it does not contain spelling, grammar, or syntax errors. It may also help to ask a trusted friend or advisor to read your personal statement and give you feedback.

Cover Letter
As a college student, you need to have a cover letter that presents the skills you have that are beneficial to the hiring organization, details the benefit you will bring to the role, and articulates your desire to work with the agency. A cover letter should be a one-page document (unless otherwise noted). Many jobs require applicants to submit a cover letter tailored to the applicant and the role you are applying for. The cover letter allows the applicant to highlight transferable skills, professional accomplishments, and academic experiences.

Generally, a cover letter begins by stating who you are and the position you are applying for. You should briefly explain why you are best suited for the job by connecting your education and experience to the company's needs. You must also state why you are interested in the organization and the role.

Your cover letter must name your skills and briefly discuss how you obtained them. For example, instead of stating, "I am proficient in Microsoft Excel," state, "In my role at XYZ company, I was responsible for creating and maintaining the company's inventory documentation system using Microsoft Excel." You want to *show,* not just *tell* your experience.

You can also discuss relevant coursework that has helped you develop specific skills, but do so briefly. End your cover letter by thanking the employer and reiterating your excitement for the opportunity and willingness to discuss the role further. Be sure to thoroughly proofread your cover letter to ensure it does not include spelling, grammar, or syntax errors. It may also help to ask a trusted friend or advisor to read your cover letter and give you feedback.

Resumé
Every college student should create a resumé demonstrating their education, skills, and work experience. Generally, organizations require applicants to submit a resumé with their application materials when they apply for internships/externships, jobs (whether full- or part-time), fellowships, and other opportunities. Your resumé is a business document that presents categories of skills and experiences in separate sections. Some of the sections included on the resume are:

- Contact information,
- Objective,
- Education,
- Experience,
- Awards and honors,
- Skills, and
- References.

Your contact information should be listed in the header of your resumé. As an entry-level applicant, you may include an "Objective" statement at the top of your resumé to indicate the value you will add to the company and the needs your skills will fulfill. In the "Education" section, present your most recent education to the oldest. Include the names of your institutions and the years you began and graduated.

If you have not graduated when applying, indicate your anticipated graduation date. Some applicants also include their GPA. In the "Work Experience" section, present your present job and list your previous jobs from the most recent to the oldest. Include the name of the company, the position you held, the year you were hired, and the year you left the company. If you are working at the company when you apply, write "present" as the end date. You can also add a brief statement describing the work you performed at the company. This statement should be no more than two sentences.

Other sections could be included on your resumé, including introduction; skills; training, certifications, and licenses; accomplishments; languages; projects; volunteer work; awards and honors; conferences, extracurricular activities; publications; hobbies and interests; relevant coursework; and fraternities or sororities.

Many employers will require applicants to submit a list of references with their application materials. It would be best if you asked people who have worked with you in your occupation or education to serve as a reference on your behalf. Potential employers will ask your reference will be asked questions such as how they know you, how long they have known you, how long they worked with you, the type of responsibilities you had, and how well you performed your duties, to name a few.

Unless you are a seasoned professional (i.e., at least five years of extensive work experience with different organizations), your resumé should be a concise, one-page document. If you choose to add any additional sections, include only relevant information highlighting the skills the company is hiring for. Each statement should be brief, because you do not want to exceed the required or suggested resumé page limit. Be sure to thoroughly proofread your resumé to ensure it does not include spelling, grammar, or syntax errors. It may also help to ask a trusted friend or advisor to read your resumé and give you feedback.

Financial Literacy Campus Resources
During college and after you secure a job, it would be beneficial to have a good grasp of your finances. Colleges have staff members who specialize in navigating grant, scholarship, financial aid, loan, and work-study processes. Get to know your financial aid representative. Your financial aid representative can assist you with learning the due dates for applications and understanding the information you need to complete your applications. As you move through the financial application processes, ask your financial aid advisor, or someone familiar with the application and the process, to review your applications before you submit each.

Many institutions also host college student financial literacy workshops to discuss the importance of credit scores, responsible credit card usage, and how to build credit, budget, and save money. College student financial literacy is an important concept that should be taught to every student. Financial literacy is the knowledge and understanding of how money works, where it comes from, and how to use it responsibly. It also involves learning about credit cards, managing debt, budgeting, saving money, investing, and more. A basic understanding of financial literacy can help you make informed decisions about your future and avoid financial crises.

As a college student, you increasingly take on large amounts of debt to fund your education. You must understand the implications of high debt levels and how to manage debt responsibly. Financial literacy can also help you decide about your future career and the costs and benefits of different career paths. Please take advantage of these learning opportunities when your institution offers them. Several important workshops to look out for include checking, savings, investment accounts, and debit card usage.

Understanding checking accounts, savings accounts, and investments are all necessary financial tools. Checking accounts allow individuals to deposit money, write checks, and make electronic payments. Checking accounts often enable easy access to debit cards, allowing customers to easily access the funds in the account without needing a paper check.

Savings accounts allow individuals to grow their money as interest is earned on the account balance. Savings accounts also provide liquidity and flexibility, allowing customers to access funds when needed. As a college student, you may use savings accounts for emergency fund deposits or long-term investment goals, such as personal or retirement savings.

Investments are another essential financial tool for you. Investment options may include stocks, bonds, mutual funds, and exchange-traded funds (ETFs). Investing provides the potential to grow money over time and can help you prepare financially for life beyond graduation. However, it is essential to remember that investments involve risk, and returns are not guaranteed. Research your options carefully before investing.

In many cases, an institution's business, accounting, finance, or management department may be able to make recommendations for professionals who could assist you in better understanding investments. Suppose your institution does not have a business department. In that case, you should research accountants and financial advisors in your area to offer you direction. It is a good idea to consult a professional specialist before making any financial or investment decisions.

The W2 Form, Payroll Deductions, and Receiving Your Wages

Many young adults begin working while in college. As such, it is essential to understand employment considerations such as what a W2 form is, the importance of paying income taxes, paycheck deductions, and how direct deposit works. A W2 form is a vital document employers must provide employees at the end of each year. It outlines an employee's total wages and the money withheld from their paycheck throughout the year to pay taxes. This information is used by the Internal Revenue Service (IRS) and the employee when they file their taxes. The W2 form lists the employer's name, employer identification number (EIN), and contact information; the employee's name, contact information, and Social Security number; and the total amounts the employee earned for wages, tips, and other compensation.

The W2 form also lists deductions for federal income tax, Social Security tax, state taxes, Medicare taxes, and 401(k) retirement contributions if these deductions were taken out of an employee's paychecks throughout the year. Paying income taxes is an essential responsibility that all employees have. Each employee should seek the help of a tax preparation professional to ensure their taxes are filed correctly and on time.

Some employees can receive their paychecks by paper check, while others will receive their wages via direct deposit. When an employee receives a paper check, they need to ether go to a financial institution to deposit the check in their account, use a mobile device to deposit the check, or cash the check to get the money. In contrast, direct deposit works by having funds electronically transferred from one bank account to another without physically transferring money between parties through cash or checks. Through direct deposit, employers can deposit wages into employees' bank accounts. Employees can access their funds using their debit card or by going to their financial institution. Employees must sign up with their employer to establish direct deposits.

As a college student, you must develop a budget to help manage your expenses in school and after graduation. Your budget needs to consider your total income and all your costs. Your total income includes all money you receive from all sources each month. Your total costs may consist of things like textbooks, housing expenses, food, clothing, electricity bill, gas bill, water bill, Internet service, cable, streaming platforms, landline and mobile phone services, laundry, miscellaneous supplies or events, the money you plan to save each month, and any other expenses you may have. It is essential to consider your budget as you are making financial decisions in college and after graduation. Be sure to download your free Budget Template from Tracy Crump Enterprises, LLC. The budget template is a great place to begin considering your expenses and learning to track your spending.

Conclusion
The various career preparation services available at an institution can prepare you for the job market. Accessing the career services office, career fairs, mock interviews, alumni association, and mentors allow you to benefit from the wealth of knowledgeable staff, former students, and industry professionals that could help you in your career search. Additionally, preparing a personal statement, cover letter, and resumé and participating in networking

Commented [JB1]: Great place for a couple examples to really show them the math -- what they earn, what the ta home amount is, and examples of how it's spent and wha might be left for their "fun money" (eating out, going out with friends/significant other, etc.)

Commented [TGC2R1]: I have a free budget template resource that I am giving readers. I am a bit hesitant to pu tax deduction estimates here because they change from year to year and differ by jurisdiction. What do you think?

opportunities will provide invaluable insight that benefits job seekers.

Activate Your A.C.E.S.

Write short phrases on the lines provided. Use the Definition Box to help you.

1. <u>A</u>chievement-driven. What is your life goal?
   a. Explain what career success looks like for you.

   _____
   _____
   _____
   _____

   _____
   _____
   _____
   _____
   _____

> **Mentor**—A trusted advisor who has experience in an area that a person is interested in learning more about and who agrees to share their knowledge.
> https://www.merriam-webster.com/dictionary/mentor
> **Financial literacy**—Understanding how to manage money, budget, and invest.
> https://www.investopedia.com/terms/f/financial-literacy.asp

2. <u>C</u>apacity-informed. What resources do you have or need to get?

a. Describe what you are currently doing to prepare for career success.

_____

_____
_____
_____
_____
_____
_____
_____
_____

3. **E**nthusiasm-oriented. What motivates you?
   a. Explain what motivates you to prepare for your career success.

_____

_____
_____
_____
_____
_____
_____
_____
_____
_____

4. **S**kill-building-focused. What current skills do you have? What skills do you need to gain?
   a. Contact your institution's career services office and get the schedule for their upcoming workshops. Attend at least 2 of your career services office's workshops.

   _____

   _____

   _____

   _____

   _____

   _____

   _____

   _____

   b. Conduct an Internet search and find three job announcements that interest you. Use these job announcements to determine the skills you need to be an ideal candidate.

   _____

   _____

   _____

_____
_____
_____
_____
_____
_____

c. List the classes or experiences you will
need to gain the skills required for the
positions.

_____
_____
_____
_____
_____
_____
_____
_____

d. Make an appointment with your career
services office to prepare your personal
statement (be sure you bring the job
announcements with you).

_____
_____

_____
_____
_____
_____
_____
_____
_____

e. Make an appointment with your career
    services office to prepare your cover letter
    (be sure you bring the job announcements
    with you).

_____
_____
_____
_____
_____
_____
_____
_____

f. Make an appointment with your career services office to prepare your resumé (be sure you bring the job announcements with you).

_____

_____

_____

_____

_____

_____

_____

_____

_____

g. List the career fairs coming up over the next six months.

_____

_____

_____

_____

_____

_____

_____

_____
_____
_____

h. Plan to attend at least one career fair.

_____
_____
_____
_____
_____
_____
_____

i. Schedule at least one mock interview session with your career services office.

_____
_____
_____
_____
_____
_____

_____
_____
_____

j. Identify 1 or 2 people you would like to serve as your personal and professional mentor.

_____
_____
_____
_____
_____
_____
_____
_____

k. List the career success resources you currently use.

_____
_____
_____
_____
_____

_____
_____
_____
_____
_____

l. List the career success resources you need
    but do not have.

_____
_____
_____
_____
_____
_____
_____
_____

m. Create an action plan to access the career
    success resources you need.

_____
_____
_____
_____

_____
_____
_____
_____
_____

n. Make an appointment with your campus
   financial aid representative or a financial
   professional to find workshops discussing
   financial literacy and managing your
   checking, savings, investment accounts,
   and debit card usage.

_____
_____
_____
_____
_____
_____
_____

o. List the financial literacy resources you
   currently have.

_____
_____

_____
_____
_____
_____
_____
_____
_____

p. List the financial literacy resources you
   need but do not have.

_____
_____
_____
_____
_____
_____
_____

q. Create an action plan to access the
   financial literacy resources you need.

_____
_____
_____

The A.C.E.S. Framework™ Check-In

Now that you know more about preparing for career success and have deepened your understanding of this topic, take what you learned and find out how it applies to your life.

Be sure to explore the related topics and resources on https://tracycrumpenterprisesllc.com/media-press.

There, you will find a wealth of information on preparing for career success, so take your time to brush up on what you have learned here and expand your knowledge.

In addition, be sure to stop by our social media pages and let us know what your three takeaways from this chapter were. Relating the material to your unique experience is one of the best ways to get started on your path to success.

TheACESFramework

@ACESFramework

www.linkedin.com/in/tracygcrump

Chapter 13
Mindfulness and Self-Care:
Keep it Cool as a Cucumber When the Heat Is On

"I matter and so do YOU! Take care of yourself."
~ Chan W., college senior

According to Barbayannis and colleagues' recent study, college students with long-term, unaddressed stress may experience poor grades, lack of motivation, and increased dropout rates. There cannot be enough said about the importance of your mental and physical health. You may experience discomfort when you leave friends and family to attend college, or you may experience challenges negotiating a new environment with new responsibilities. When obstacles challenge your mental health or physical well-being, there are strategies you can use to monitor your mental hygiene and mindfully engage in self-care.

Addressing Homesickness
It is common for people to miss home when they move to a new environment. This may also be true for you. In some cases, students experience an emotional discomfort caused by being away from home or separated from loved ones—homesickness. This feeling can be distressing and

especially difficult to cope with due to the transition into a new environment and lifestyle. Although it is typical for college students to feel homesick at some point during their first year, if this happens to you, you can use several strategies to address this emotion healthily.

As a college student, you can schedule time with family and friends and set times and days to contact them before you go away to school or move. You must stay in contact with friends and family back home, because this will help them maintain connections while you are away. Additionally, you can engage in activities that remind you of home, such as eating your favorite foods or joining a school club or sport that you participated in before. Furthermore, you can maintain an open dialogue with peers and fellow students at the college to boost your morale and provide support. If homesickness becomes overwhelming, seek professional help from a counselor at the institution's counseling center.

Monitor Your Mental Hygiene
When attempting to understand ourselves and each other, human beings often desire distinct categories with explainable experiences. However, there are many gray areas when we explore the essential questions about our world and the people experiencing this journey with us. We find that lived experience is different. Some experiences are difficult to confront because they may be beautiful and painful or exhausting and energizing. It is essential to realize that life is full of contradictions, as are people's experiences. Monitoring your mental hygiene includes examining how you feel mentally, emotionally,

and physically each day and assessing all measures you can take to promote and preserve your mental health.

The college experience includes several potentially stressful elements, including:

- living away from family and support systems,
- managing an increased workload,
- having competing responsibilities,
- personal pressure due to self-expectations,
- expectations of others,
- financial worries,
- relationship pressures,
- difficulty concentrating,
- worrying about future success, and
- others.

If left unaddressed, stress could have a negative physical impact, including resulting in mood swings because of being unable to regulate emotions, experiencing changes in appetite, feeling overwhelmed, exhibiting mental health challenges, exhaustion, headaches, experiencing low energy, upset stomach, diarrhea, constipation, nausea, having feelings of hopelessness, experiencing aches and pains, having tense muscles, being unable to sleep, and others.

So, it is crucial for you to monitor your mental hygiene and not let college stressors get out of control so it does not wear your body down and lead to severe psychological and physical health issues. There are several mindfulness strategies you can use to decrease stress and engage in self-care.

Use Self-Care Strategies

You can do several things to have stress relief at your fingertips. For example, as discussed in Chapter 8, developing a sound time-management system will help with procrastination and feeling overburdened or overbooked. Art therapy can help a student who likes to draw, use graphics, or take photos. Some students may enjoy keeping a journal. Listening to your favorite music could also be a form of music therapy that decreases stress. You may benefit from using aromatherapy as a stress reliever. Additionally, ensuring that you are hydrated, eating a healthier diet, and moving your body can help with mood, brain fog, and fatigue.

Furthermore, it helps to speak and walk in your truth. Choose what to say no to and then say *no*. You can also recognize there are some things that you cannot change. If there is something in your life that you cannot change, look for a way to take yourself out of the situation or get extra help. It may be challenging, but it will go a long way toward managing your physical and emotional safety. There are ways to cope with difficult circumstances and find support. Do not hesitate to ask for help when needed. With the right approach, you can make a difficult situation more manageable. To stay on track, you should make it a practice to avoid harmful behaviors and unhealthy relationships.

Remember that laughter is a great healer. When you can take in a good comedy, watch a movie, go to a comedy show, or laugh with friends or family, do it, because it can help relieve stress. Using positive affirmations also is very helpful. This is called the psychological counterpunch. Suppose you wake up every morning and tell yourself you are brilliant and beautiful and here to change the world. In that case, it would be difficult for someone else to tell you otherwise.

It would help if you also avoid procrastination. People often feel overwhelmed when they have put something off until it cannot be shelved any longer. Be sure to schedule your time, because not doing so increases stress. Another stress reliever is to unplug from technology. Sometimes you need to be alone with your thoughts. So, you want to give yourself time away from your technology and unplug. Be sure to schedule your time so you can get enough sleep. This can be challenging, but most people need eight sustained hours of sleep daily. Another helpful technique to address the need for sleep may be to take a power nap.

Similarly, you want to take mental health breaks and take advantage of your alone time. Practicing mindfulness by taking several deep breaths for a few minutes to get fresh oxygen in your lungs may be helpful. In some cases, sitting alone with your thoughts may help. In other cases, being surrounded by beautiful scenery and getting fresh air could be a benefit. Whatever it is for you, take advantage of mindfulness and relaxation techniques. There are several free mindfulness apps available.

Another strategy is to lean on your support system. You always want to have a team that you can go to, whether it is a friend, a family member, an associate, or someone more professional like a counselor, a psychiatrist, or a therapist. Make sure that you have access to someone you can talk to when you need to talk, and always ask for help when you need it. So, you want to constantly monitor your emotional, social, intellectual, spiritual, physical, environmental, and occupational wellness. Remember: You can decrease your stress and make positive things happen.

Conclusion
Obstacles will be present throughout life, but you must monitor how you feel mentally and physically each day. You will be required to navigate new environments and unfamiliar circumstances. Still, you can use mindfulness and self-care techniques to help decrease life's stressors. You can also ask for help from trusted friends, family members, or mental health professionals.

Activate Your A.C.E.S.

Write short phrases on the lines provided. Use the Definition Box to help you.

> **Mindfulness**—Being fully present in the moment and devoting attention to one's current environment.
> https://www.mindful.org/what-is-mindfulness/
>
> **Self-Care**—A person's ability to make healthy lifestyle choices.
> https://www.everydayhealth.com/self-care/

1. **A**chievement-driven. What is your life goal?
   a. Explain your mindfulness and self-care goals.

   _____
   _____

   _____
   _____
   _____
   _____
   _____
   _____
   _____

2. **C**apacity-informed. What resources do you have or need to get?
   a. Describe how you currently engage in mindfulness and self-care.

   _____
   _____

   _____

_____
_____
_____
_____
_____
_____
_____

3. **E**nthusiasm-oriented. What motivates you?
   a. Explain what motivates you to engage in mindfulness and self-care.

_____
_____
_____
_____
_____
_____
_____
_____

4. **S**kill-building-focused. What current skills do you have? What skills do you need to gain?
   a. List the people you want to remain in contact with when you begin college and set a day and time you will be available to

connect with them (the days and times can be different for each week or month).

_____
_____
_____
_____
_____
_____
_____
_____

b. Write the names and contact information of the people in your support system that you can call if you need someone to talk to.

_____
_____
_____
_____
_____
_____
_____
_____

c. List your favorite foods and enjoy one at
    least once a month.

    _____

    _____

    _____

    _____

    _____

    _____

    _____

d. List your favorite songs and listen to them
    during downtime or while commuting
    throughout your day.

    _____

    _____

    _____

    _____

    _____

    _____

    _____

e. List your favorite activities and do at least one thing per week.

_____

_____

_____

_____

_____

_____

_____

f. List your favorite movies or shows and watch one at least once each week.

_____

_____

_____

_____

_____

_____

_____

g. List your favorite books and have some on hand if you have downtime to read for enjoyment (listening to audiobooks may be a good idea if you want to listen to your books while commuting or doing something else).

_____

_____

_____

_____

_____

_____

_____

_____

h. List the days and times you will exercise and add them to your schedule.

_____

_____

_____

_____

_____

_____

_____

_____

i. Write down your institution's counseling center's e-mail, telephone number, physical address, and hours of operation if you need to contact them.

_____

_____
_____
_____
_____
_____
_____
_____
_____

j. Write down the name, e-mail address, telephone number, physical address, and hours of operation of your primary care physician and any other medical or mental health personnel you routinely see.

_____

_____
_____
_____
_____

_____
_____
_____

k. List the mindfulness and self-care
    resources you currently have.

_____
_____
_____
_____
_____
_____
_____
_____

l. List the mindfulness and self-care
    resources you need but do not have.

_____
_____
_____
_____
_____
_____

_____
_____

m. Create an action plan to access the mindfulness and self-care resources you need.

_____
_____
_____
_____
_____
_____
_____
_____
_____

The A.C.E.S. Framework™ Check-In

Now that you know more about mindfulness and self-care and have deepened your understanding of this topic, take what you learned and find out how it applies to your life.

Be sure to explore the related topics and resources on https://tracycrumpenterprisesllc.com/media-press.

There, you will find a wealth of information on mindfulness and self-care, so take your time to brush up on what you have learned here and expand your knowledge.

In addition, be sure to stop by our social media pages and let us know what your three takeaways from this chapter were. Relating the material to your unique experience is one of the best ways to get started on your path to success.

TheACESFramework

@ACESFramework

www.linkedin.com/in/tracygcrump

Afterword
WHEW! You've Arrived

I hope the lessons in *A.C.E.S. for Students: Strategies for Success in the First Year of College & Beyond* have given you more clarity about yourself, your goals, and your skill set. I wrote the book because, as a first-generation college student, I did not have a clear direction on courses to take, resources to access, my goals and requirements, or the connections I needed to make to successfully prepare for my career. Truthfully, I did not know the career path that would best fit me. Due to my lack of clarity, I experienced a lot of challenges that I could have avoided had I know more about myself and my goals. I could have greatly benefitted from having a book like A.C.E.S. for Students.

For almost two decades, I have counseled students and families who struggled with similar clarity issues. I want to do my part in eliminating the intrapersonal barriers to college access, retention, and graduation that some students face. In writing this book, my goal is to help 1,000,000 students confidently enter college knowing their goals, understanding their resources, and feeling prepared to seize their destiny by activating their A.C.E.S.™ Each chapter in *A.C.E.S. for Students* was designed to help students better understand their unique mix of goals, needs, and resources. After completing the "Activate Your A.C.E.S." sections, you will have a much better understanding of the following:

- your emotional intelligence and how to use it in various scenarios,
- your self-identity and how to express yourself confidently,
- your motivations, preferred learning styles, and learning methods for more effective studying,
- the strategies you can use to make the most of college resources,
- your expectations when it comes to personal and professional relationships with faculty and staff,
- the techniques you need for successful college readiness preparations
- effective time and task management strategies for staying organized and on track,
- your plan for how to make the most of your faculty and staff knowledge,
- your career search strategy,
- how to tap into your leadership potential, and
- what is needed to take care of yourself mentally and physically.

Congratulations on taking the next step on your life's journey. I wish you all the success life offers, and I cannot wait to see the excellent work you will do!

Acknowledgments [I'm still working on this]

One thing I know for sure is that my village has been, and will always be, my foundation and the reason I am able to do the work I do. For that I say thank you to:

- The ancestors whose name I do not know but whose blood runs through my veins, fuels my passions, and grounds me through the chaos.
- Louise A. Simmons and John A. Grayer for showing me that I can persist despite all challenges and obstacles.
- Betty G. Jackson who is my biggest cheer leader, my first teacher, and the person taught me that I could be anything I want to be.
- Ronald Hickey for showing me unconditional love and teaching me that familial bonds can transcend biology, time, and space.
- Richard D. Jackson for guiding me into adulthood and loving me through my flaws.
- Rufus R. Smith, Jr. for teaching me about agency and showing me how to stand on my own.
- Stephanie R. Clayton
- Louise A. Guice
- Carl Guice for being a constant reminder of
- Kenneth Guice
- Christina Guice
- Joe N. Grayer, Sr.
- Mellody Stroy
- Joe N. Grayer, Jr.
- Vanessa Bishop

- Olivia Bell for loving the sweetest little girl and giving me the opportunity to continue to prepare for her future.
- Amanda Butler for standing in the gap
- Julia Humphrey
- Yavonka Muhammad for showing me
- Keisha Manning Cal
- Vernetta Washington for giving me a space to grow and dream when the world seemed to spin out of control.
- Nora Washington
- Debra Washington
- Juanita Ford
- Leslie Fulton for teaching me what compassionate leadership looked and felt like.
- Stella Guzman
- Althea McCraven
- Yvonne Isom for being my listening ear, a sounding board, and the voice of reason.
- Ashley N. Kirkwood for teaching me how important it is to use my voice and tell my story.
- Iman Saca
- Sonya Malunda for showing me how to create my own seat at the table.
- Michelle Obama
- Mary Carol Ghislin
- Jodi Bandon
- Ida Fia Sveningsson for translating the vision in my head to a vision the world can experience.
- Devon Kidd

Teachers/mentors/bosses

- Charles Davis for showing me that dynamic teachers who look like me do exist and can change the world for the better.
- Ms. Barker for teaching me to dream bigger than my surroundings
- Doug Thomson for seeing the teacher in me before I knew she existed.
- Beth E. Richie for being my mentor and Inspirations
- The graduating classes of Hyde Park Career Academy 1993, Chicago State University 2004 and 2006, the University of Illinois Chicago (UIC) 2012, the Loyola University Continuing and Professional Studies 2013, the University of Chicago Law School 2016, and the Loyola University Chicago School of Law 2016.
- Every student I ever taught and learned from

I want to thank God for giving the people I mentioned above the fortitude to deal with me.

Informational Page

Click the 📷 below ✋ to visit our website 🌐, check out our services ⛅, and partner with us 🤝 to move one step closer to your EMPOWERED FUTURE.

https://tracycrumpenterprisesllc.com/

https://tracycrumpenterprisesllc.com/book

Stay in touch with us on social media

LinkedIn
www.linkedin.com/in/tracygcrump

Instagram
TheACESFramework

Twitter
@ACESFramework

How to continue to work with me

Join my mailing list
Be on the lookout for posts and articles on my LinkedIn page

Enroll in my online A.C.E.S for students course
Book me as an orientation speaker
Enroll in my workshops
Book me as a keynote speaker

References

Anderson, J. C., & Kleiner, B. H. (2021). Benefits of

effective forecasting, planning and

     scheduling. *Industrial Management, 63*(4), 16–

21.

Anderson, M., & Lu, F. (2017, March 8). *Research: How*

leadership experience affects students.

Harvard Business Review. Retrieved February 3, 2023, from https://hbr.org/2017/02/research-how-leadership-experience-affects-students.

Arif, H., Khan, M. U., & Abbas, Q. (2021). Grit and its related factors in undergraduate students.
Pakistan Journal of Clinical Psychology, 20(2), 3–20.

Baba, Y., & Hosoda, M. (2014). Home away home: Better understanding of the role of social
support in predicting cross-cultural adjustment among international students. *College Student Journal, 48*(1), 1–15.

Barbayannis, G., Bandari, M., Zheng, X., Baquerizo, H., Pecor, K. W., & Ming, X. (2022).
Academic Stress and Mental Well-Being in College Students: Correlations, Affected Groups,

and COVID-19. *Frontiers in psychology, 13,*

886344.

Barger, T. S. (2018, November 26). *College orientation:*

Making an impact. University Business.

Retrieved February 3, 2023, from

https://universitybusiness.com/college-

orientation-making-an-impact/.

Bartlett, J. A. (2022). Beyond the to-do list: Personal

knowledge management tools and

techniques. *Kentucky Libraries, 86*(2), 4–7.

Benjamin, A. S., & Tullis, J. (2010) What makes

distributed practice effective? *Cognitive*

Psychology, 61, 228–247.

Bigouette, J. P., Ford, L., Segaloff, H. E., Langolf, K.,

Kahrs, J., Zochert, T., Tate, J. E., Gieryn,

D., Kirking, H. L., Westergaard, R. P., &

Killerby, M. E. (2021). Association of shared

living spaces and COVID-19 in university

students, Wisconsin, USA, 2020. *Emerging*

*Infectious Diseases, 27(*11), 2882–2886.

Bowman, N. A., & Levtov, A. H. (2020). Understanding
and using growth mindset to foster

college student learning and achievement. *New*

Directions for Teaching & Learning, 2020(164),

75–83.

Branca, S. H., & Slusser, E. (2022). Through a more
discerning lens: Understanding college

student expectations and experiences over the

course of a semester. *College Student Journal,*

56(2), 180–196.

Cai, L. (2022). Effect of physical exercise intervention based on improved neural network on

    college students' mental health. *Computational & Mathematical Methods in Medicine*, 1–9.

Chakroborty, S., & Vohra, N. (2021). Relationship between social safeness and resilience

    amongst college students: An empirical study. *Indian Journal of Positive Psychology, 12*(4), 392–396.

Chen, P.-H. (2021). In-class and after-class lecture note-taking strategies. *Active Learning in Higher Education, 22*(3), 245–260.

Cherry, H. (2022, June 17). *Here's how your identity and sense of self affect your growth.*

    Forbes. Retrieved February 2, 2023, from https://www.forbes.com/sites/womensmedia/202

2/06/16/heres-how-your-personal-identity-and-

sense-of-self-affect-your-

growth/?sh=33a5ec0e69bf.

Cirillo, F. (2018). *The pomodoro technique: The*

acclaimed time-management system that has

transformed how we work. New York, NY:

Currency-Penguin Random House Books.

Clough, B. A., Nazareth, S. M., & Casey, L. M. (2020).

Making the grade: a pilot investigation

of an e-intervention to increase mental health

literacy and help-seeking intentions among

international university students. *British Journal*

of Guidance & Counselling, 48(3), 347–359.

Crews, D. C., Wilson, K. L., Sohn, J., Kabacoff, C. M.,

Poynton, S. L., Murphy, L. R., Bolz, J.,

Wolfe, A., White, P. T., Will, C., Collins, C., Gauda, E., & Robinson, D. N. (2020). Helping scholars overcome socioeconomic barriers to medical and biomedical careers: Creating a pipeline initiative. *Teaching & Learning in Medicine, 32*(4), 422–433.

Crump, T. G. (2021, April 22). Providing virtual legal writing support to law students beyond the classroom. LWI. Retrieved March 6, 2023, from https://www.lwionline.org/article/providing-virtual-legal-writing-support-law-students-beyond-classroom

de Prada Creo, E., Mareque, M., & Portela-Pino, I. (2021). The acquisition of teamwork skills in university students through extra-curricular activities. *Education + Training, 63*(2), 165–181.

Deris, F. D., Hasan, N., & Noor, N. A. M. (2021).
Mentor-mentee as a strategy to increase
willingness to communicate among student
leaders: A case study. *E-BANGI Journal, 18*(8),
119–135.

Devaraj, D., & Ahmad, M. (2022). Effects of music
therapy on psychological distress of
neurosurgical patients: A systematic review.
*Malaysian Journal of Health Sciences / Jurnal
Sains Kesihatan Malaysia, 20*(1), 73–81.

Dey, F., & Cruzvergara, C. Y. (2014). Evolution of
career services in higher education. *New
Directions for Student Services, 2014*(148), 5–18.

Driver, P., Caldwell, T. L., & Grunert, L. (2023).
Exploring UTA effectiveness: Leveraging

undergraduate teaching assistants for student

learning and help-seeking. *Teaching of*

Psychology, 50(1), 57–68.

Eichelberger, B., Gerbing, D., & Gillpatrick, T. (2019).
Financial education, college retention,

and graduation rates. *College Student Journal,*

53(4), 479–489.

Erlandson, K. (2014). Sexiled: Privacy acquisition
strategies of college roommates. *Journal of*

College & University Student Housing, 41(1),

12–29.

Fay, M. P., Jaggars, S. S., & Farakish, N. (2022). "Lost
in the shuffle": How relationships and

personalized advisement shape transfer

aspirations and outcomes for community college

students. *Community College Review, 50*(4),
366–390.

Finn, D. (2022). Online learning and universal design:
Practical applications for reaching adult
learners. *COABE Journal: The Resource for
Adult Education, 11*(1), 101–109.

Geller, J., Toftness, A. R., Armstrong, P. I., Carpenter, S.
K., Manz, C. L., Coffman, C. R., &
Lamm, M. H. (2018). Study strategies and beliefs
about learning as a function of academic
achievement and achievement goals. *Memory,
26*(5), 683–690.

Georgiev, D. (2023, January 26). *20+ little-known time
management statistics for 2023.*

Techjury. Retrieved February 3, 2023, from
https://techjury.net/blog/time-management-
statistics/#gref.

Gierke, L., Binder, N., Heckmann, M., Odağ, Ö., Leiser,
A., & Kedzior, K. K. (2018). Definition
of intercultural competence (IC) in undergraduate
students at a private university in the USA: A
mixed-methods study. *PLoS ONE, 13*(4), 1–17.

Gilmore, C. (2021, June 25). *How your student support
services can improve retention.*
EducationDynamics. Retrieved February 3, 2023,
from https://www.educationdynamics.com/how-
your-student-support-services-can-improve-
retention/#:~:text=Student%20support%20servic
es%20help%20keep,pushing%20and%20achieve
%20their%20goals.

Gu, X. (2022). Effect of Deep Learning on College

Students' Career Planning. *Mathematical*

    Problems in Engineering, 1–12.

https://doi.org/10.1155/2022/1573635

Gupta, N., & Kumar, S. (2015). Significant predictors for

resilience among a sample of

    undergraduate students: Acceptance, forgiveness

    and gratitude. *Indian Journal of Health &*

    Wellbeing, 6(2), 188–191.

Harper, C. E., Zhu, H., & Marquez Kiyama, J. (2020).

Parents and families of first-generation

    college students experience their own college

    transition. *Journal of Higher Education, 91*(4),

    540–564.

Harris, B. R., & Maher, B. M. (2022). Student-athlete

mental health, help-seeking, and service

utilization: Implications for a multi-tiered, public

health approach on college campuses. *Journal of*

College Student Psychotherapy, 1–20.

Hasan, G. (2019). Formal structures of mentorship in

universities and research institutions will

benefit both science and scientists. *Current*

Science (00113891), 116(10), 1615–1616.

He, Z., Zhou, Y., Li, F., Rao, Z., & Yang, Y. (2021). The

effect of proactive personality on

college students' career decision-making

difficulties: Moderating and mediating effects.

Journal of Adult Development, 28(2), 116–125.

Henninger IV, W. R., Eshbaugh, E. M., OsbeckS, A., &

Madigan, C. (2016). Perceived social

support and roommate status as predictors of

college student loneliness. *Journal of College &*

University Student Housing, 42(2), 46–59.

Hidayat, L., Huggins, C. E., Venugopalan, V., &

Berrios-Colon, E. (2017). Preparing students to

enter the race for postgraduate training. *Journal*

of Pharmacy Practice, 30(4), 476–482.

Hudson, T. D., Rockenbach, A. N., & Mayhew, M. J.

(2022). Campus conditions and college

experiences that facilitate friendship across

worldview differences. *Journal of Higher*

Education, 1–29.

Jacoby, B. (2015). Enhancing commuter student success:

What's theory got to do with it? *New*

Directions for Student Services, 2015(150), 3–12.

Jaeschke, A., & Morrison, R. (2021, January 15). School vs. life: Expert tips on setting (and

defending) your boundaries. CampusWell. Retrieved February 3, 2023, from https://www.campuswell.com/time-management-for-college-students/.

Johnston, B. M. 2021. Students as partners: Peer-leading in an undergraduate mathematics

course. *International Journal of Mathematical Education in Science & Technology 52*(5): 795–806.

Julien S. Bureau, Joshua L. Howard, Jane X. Y. Chong, and Frédéric Guay. (2021). Pathways to

Student Motivation: A Meta-Analysis of Antecedents of Autonomous and Controlled

Motivations. *Review of Educational Research,*

92(1), 46–72.

Kalyanasundaram, M., Abraham, S. B., Ramachandran,

D., Bazroy, J., Singh, Z., Purty, A. J., &

Jayaseelan, V. (2017). Effectiveness of mind

mapping technique in information retrieval

among medical college students in Puducherry: A

pilot study. *Indian Journal of Community*

Medicine, 42(1), 19–23.

Khan, M., Minbashian, A., & MacCann, C. (2021).

College students in the western world are

becoming less emotionally intelligent: A cross-

temporal meta-analysis of trait emotional

intelligence. *Journal of Personality, 89*(6), 1176–

1190.

Kokkoris, M. D., & Sedikides, C. (2019). Can you be
yourself in business? How reminders of

business affect the perceived value of

authenticity. *Journal of Applied Social
Psychology, 49*(7), 448–458.

Kulkarni, B., Banerjee, R., & Raghunathan, R.

(2022). Why students should be taught

differently: learner characteristics, learning styles

and simulation performance. *Simulation &
Gaming, 53*(1), 56–74.

Laemmli, T., Grodsky, E., & Macgregor, L. C. (2022).
Going places: First-generation college

students framing higher education. *Sociological

Forum, 37*(4), 972–994.

Laidlaw, A., McLellan, J., & Ozakinci, G. (2016).
Understanding undergraduate student

perceptions of mental health, mental well-being

and help-seeking behaviour. *Studies in Higher*

Education, 41(12), 2156–2168.

Landa, I., Bono, T. J., & English, T. (2020). Mood
regulation and relationship quality predict

change in homesickness during college. *British*

Journal of Psychology, 111(1), 55–69.

Lastiri, L. (2022, August 13). What is productivity for
students? (9 ways to increase it). Iris

Reading. Retrieved February 3, 2023, from

https://irisreading.com/what-is-productivity-for-

students-9-ways-to-increase-

it/#:~:text=It%20is%20a%20measure%20of,inpu

t%20into%20achieving%20academic%20success

.

Lei, S. A. (2015). Variation in study patterns among college students: A review of literature.

    College Student Journal, 49(2), 195–198.

Lei, S. A., & Yin, D. (2019). Evaluating benefits and drawbacks of internships: Perspectives of

    college students. *College Student Journal, 53*(2), 181–189.

Levine, S.C., Reimers, T., & Hulleman, C.S (2005). Mind-sets matter: A meta-analytic review of

    implicit theories and self-regulation. *Psychological Bulletin 131*(3), 300–329.

Li, L. (2022). Effects of aerobic exercise on sleep quality and mental health of college students.

    Occupational Therapy International, 1–9.

Loi, N. M., & Pryce, N. (2022). The role of mindful self-care in the relationship between emotional intelligence and burnout in university

students. *Journal of Psychology, 156*(4), 295–

309.

López Vergara, C. C. (2022). Creating a competitive

advantage for a successful career trajectory.

Journal of Multidisciplinary Research (1947-

2900), 14(2), 77–84.

Martinez, E., & Elue, C. (2020). From community

college to graduate school: Exploring the role

of academic advisors in promoting graduate

education at baccalaureate degree-granting

community colleges. *Journal of Higher*

Education, 91(7), 1003–1027.

Mason, C. P., Dye, L., & Mason-Bennett, L. (2022).

Mindfulness strategies for helping college

students manage stress: A guide for higher

education professionals. *International Journal of*

Choice Theory & Reality Therapy, 42(1), 82–90.

Mayer, R. E., & Anderson, R. B. (1992). The instructive

animation: Helping students build

connections between words and pictures in

multimedia learning. *Journal of Educational*

Psychology, 4, 444–452.

McDaniel, M. A., & Donnelly, C. M. (1996). Learning

with analogy and elaborative

interrogation. *Journal of Educational*

Psychology, 88, 508–519.

McMurray, A., Scott, D., & Simmers, C. A. (2019).

Work values ethic and personal

discretionary non-work activities. *International*

Journal of Manpower, 40(4), 704–716.

Meng, Q., Zhang, J., Kang, J., & Wu, Y. (2020). Effects of sound environment on the sleep of

    college students in China. *Science of the Total Environment, 705*, N.PAG.

Menon, A., & Nakhat, P. (2020). Emotional intelligence in college students. *Journal of*

    Psychosocial Research, 15(2), 575–587.

Milovanska-Farrington, S. (2020). Reasons to attend college, academic success, and post-college

    plans. *Education Economics, 28*(5), 526–547.

Morehead, K., Dunlosky, J., Rawson, K. A., Blasiman, R., & Hollis, R. B. (2019). Note-taking

    habits of 21st century college students: implications for student learning, memory, and achievement. *Memory, 27*(6), 807–819.

Nistor, N., Daxecker, I., Stanciu, D., & Diekamp, O. (2015). Sense of community in academic communities of practice: predictors and effects. *Higher Education (00181560), 69*(2), 257–273.

Pace, K., Silk, K., Nazione, S., Fournier, L., & Collins-Eaglin, J. (2018). Promoting mental health help-seeking behavior among first-year college students. *Health Communication, 33*(2), 102–110.

Pauk, W., & Owens, R. J. Q. (2010). *How to study in college* (10 ed.). Boston, MA: Wadsworth. ISBN 978-1-4390-8446-5. Chapter 10: "The Cornell System: Take Effective Notes", pp. 235–277.

Pence, A. R., & Dymond, S. K. (2015). Extracurricular school clubs: A time for fun and learning. *Teaching Exceptional Children, 47*(5), 281–288.

Perry, A. (2022). Nourished for a lifetime. *Christianity Today,* 85–100.

Petty, T. (2014). Motivating first-generation students to academic success and college

   completion. *College Student Journal, 48*(2), 257–264.

Price, E. W., & Swan, A. M. (2020). Connecting, coping, and creating: An expressive arts group

   for first year college students. *Journal of Creativity in Mental Health, 15*(3), 378–392.

Putnam, A. L., Victor W. Sungkhasettee, and III, Henry L. Roediger. 2016. Optimizing learning in college: Tips from cognitive

Psychology. *Perspectives on Psychological*

Science 11(5): 652–60.

Ranney, M., Kleinpeter, C. B., & Potts, M. (2018).

Personal wellbeing, depression, and alcohol

use among community college students receiving

services from a student health center.

International Journal of Health, Wellness &

Society, 8(2), 43–50.

Raposa, E. B., Hagler, M., Liu, D., & Rhodes, J. E.

(2021). Predictors of close faculty–student

relationships and mentorship in higher education:

findings from the Gallup–Purdue Index. *Annals*

of the New York Academy of Sciences, 1483(1),

36–49.

Rawson, K. A., Thomas, R. C., & Jacoby, L. L. (2014).
The power of examples: Illustrative

    examples enhance conceptual learning of

    declarative concepts. *Educational Psychology*

    Review, 27, 483–504.

Roediger, H. L., Putnam, A. L., & Smith, M. A. (2011).
Ten benefits of testing and their

    applications to educational practice. In J. Mestre

    & B. Ross (Eds.), *Psychology of learning and*

    motivation: Cognition in Education (pp. 1–36).

    Oxford: Elsevier.

Rohrer, D. (2012). Interleaving helps students
distinguish among similar concepts. *Educational*

    Psychology Review, 24, 355–367.

Rosch, D. M., & Collins, J. D. (2017). Chapter 1: The
significance of student organizations to

leadership development. *New Directions for Student Leadership, 2017*(155), 9–19.

Roy, B. D. (2022, October 12). *Understanding and utilizing emotional intelligence in the workplace*. Nurture an Engaged and Satisfied Workforce | Vantage Circle HR Blog. Retrieved February 2, 2023, from https://blog.vantagecircle.com/emotional-intelligence-in-the-workplace/#:~:text=Emotional%20Intelligence%20is%20responsible%20for,%241%2C300%20to%20an%20annual%20salary.

Sanchez-Rodriguez, N. A., & LoGiudice, J. (2018). Building bridges: Fostering dynamic partnerships between the library department and office of student disability services in higher education. *Journal of Access Services, 15*(4), 142–160.

Sarabia, H., Enriquez, L. E., Rodriguez, V. E., Zaragoza, L., & Tinoco, S. (2021). What helps students get help?: An exploratory analysis of factors that shape undocumented college students' use of academic support services. *Journal of Latinos & Education, 20*(3), 290–303.

Shell, M. D., & Absher, T. N. (2019). Effects of shyness and friendship on socioemotional adjustment during the college transition. *Personal Relationships, 26*(3), 386–405.

Shell, M. D., Shears, D., & Millard, Z. (2020). Who am I? Identity development during the first year of college. *Psi Chi Journal of Psychological Research, 25*(2), 192–202.

Sparks, S. D. (2021, September 17). *Why teacher-student relationships matter*. EducationWeek.

Retrieved February 3, 2023, from

https://www.edweek.org/teaching-learning/why-

teacher-student-relationships-

matter/2019/03#:~:text=A%20Review%20of%20

Educational%20Research,fewer%20disruptive%2

0behaviors%20and%20suspensions%2C.

Stewart, C. (2022). Universal design for learning in adult literacy education increasing outcomes

for all learners. *COABE Journal: The Resource for Adult Education, 11*(1), 135–139.

Stone, C., Trisi, D., Sherman, A., & Beltrán, J. (2020, January 13). A guide to statistics on

historical trends in income inequality. Center on Budget and Policy Priorities. Retrieved February

3, 2023, from

https://www.cbpp.org/research/poverty-and-inequality/a-guide-to-statistics-on-historical-trends-in-income-inequality.

Stonebraker, I., Maybee, C., & Chapman, J. (2019). Undergraduate students' experiences of using information at the career fair: A phenomenographic study conducted by the libraries and career center. *Journal of Academic Librarianship, 45*(4), 358–367.

Stoner, J. C. (2018). Moving the needle on residential GPAs: A thought experiment exploring the potential impact of course-specific academic support initiatives. *Journal of College & University Student Housing, 45*(1), 10–25.

Tagirova, N. P., Yudina, A. M., Krasnova, L. N.,

Gorbunov, M. A., Shelevoi, D. G., Spirina, E.

    V., & Lisitsyna, T. B. (2020). Mentoring in

    higher education: Aspect of innovative practices

    interaction in development of student

    professional and personal competencies.

    EurAsian Journal of Biosciences, 14(2), 3617–

    3623.

Thinknetic. (2022). *The art of note taking: Your*

research-based guide to taking notes that will

    stick to your memory. Thinknetic.

Thomas, L. (2020). "I am happy just doing the work ..."

Commuter student engagement in the

    wider higher education experience. *Higher*

Education Quarterly, 74(3), 290–303.

Tseng, H., Kuo, Y.-C., & Walsh, E. J. (2020). Exploring first-time online undergraduate and
    graduate students' growth mindsets and flexible thinking and their relations to online learning engagement. *Educational Technology Research & Development, 68*(5), 2285–2303.

von Suchodoletz, A., Rahn, J., Nadyukova, I., Barza, L., & Achtziger, A. (2020). Can mindsets
    influence college students' motivation to learn? Findings from the United States and the United Arab Emirates. *Higher Education (00181560), 79*(4), 731–748.

Wang, T. R. (2014). Formational turning points in the transition to college: Understanding how
    communication events shape first-generation students' pedagogical and interpersonal

relationships with their college teachers.

Communication Education, 63(1), 63–82.

Weijden, I., Belder, R., Arensbergen, P., & Besselaar, P.
(2015). How do young tenured

professors benefit from a mentor? Effects on

management, motivation and performance.

Higher Education (00181560), 69(2), 275–287.

Wolfinbarger, K. G., Shehab, R. L., Trytten, D. A., &
Walden, S. E. (2021). The influence of

engineering competition team participation on

students' leadership identity development.

Journal of Engineering Education, 110(4), 925–

948.

Wolters, C. A., & Brady, A. C. (2021). College students'
time management: A self-regulated

learning perspective. *Educational Psychology*

Review, 33(4), 1319–1351.

Wong, B. Y. L. (1985). Self-questioning instructional

research: A review. *Review of Educational*

Research, 55, 227–268.

Wurtz, K. A. (2015). Impact of learning assistance center

utilization on success. *Journal of*

Developmental Education, 38(3), 2–10.

Young-Jones, A., Levesque, C., Fursa, S., & McCain, J.

(2021). Autonomy-supportive language

in the syllabus: supporting students from the first

day. *Teaching in Higher Education, 26*(4), 541–

556.

Ziomek-Daigle, J. (2017). Using reflective writing

practices to articulate student learning in

counselor education. *Journal of Creativity in Mental Health, 12*(2), 262–270.